Maharishi's Yoga: The Royal Path to Enlightenment

William F. Sands, PhD

Maharishi University of Management Press
Fairfield, Iowa USA

© William F. Sands 2013 All rights reserved.

Published by
Maharishi University of Management Press
Fairfield, Iowa, United States of America

No part of this publication may be reproduced, stored in a retrieval system, or transmitted, in any form or by any means, electronic, mechanical, photocopying, recording, or otherwise, without the prior permission of the author.

ISBN: 978-0-923569-48-8

® Transcendental Meditation, TM-Sidhi, and Maharishi Ayur-Veda are registered or common law trademarks licensed to Maharishi Foundation USA and used under sublicense.

Acknowledgments

I am deeply grateful to Dr. Craig Pearson for his kind attention and insightful comments, and for his generosity in sharing his wealth of knowledge about writing. I would also like to express my deep gratitude to Dr. Susan Brown for her excellent suggestions and to Dr. Patricia Oates for her careful review of the text and discerning comments. I'm also grateful to Dr. Dara Llewellyn for her editorial recommendations, and to Fran Clark for her invaluable attention to both large concepts and fine details. And finally I would like to thank Harry Bright for his continued wisdom and support.

Maharishi Mahesh Yogi

Founder
The Transcendental Meditation Program
The TM-Sidhi Program
Maharishi University of Management

"Here is a technique that enables every man to come to the great treasure house within himself and so rise above all sorrows and uncertainties in life."

— Maharishi

Table of Contents

Introduction 1

Chapter 1: The State of Yoga 5
    Arjuna's dilemma 5
    Lord Krishna's advice 7
    Freed from duality, ever firm in purity, and independent of
    possessions 14
    The inner Self in the Upanishads 16

Chapter 2: The Path of Yoga 19
    What is Transcendental Meditation practice? 21
    How the Transcendental Meditation program works 22
    Research comparing different meditations 25

Chapter 3: The Experience of Yoga 27
    Experiences of pure consciousness in the Upanishads 27
    Research on Transcendental Meditation practice 31
    A state of deep rest 32
    Increased wakefulness and a more orderly brain 34
    Periods of natural respiratory suspension 36
    Frequency of pure consciousness experiences 36

Chapter 4: Yoga and the Development of Mental Potential 39
    The human brain 40
    Research on the Transcendental Meditation program and
    mental potential 42
    Growth of intelligence 43

Chapter 5: Yoga and Health 48
    Stress 48
    Stress in students' lives 49
    Transcendental Meditation practice and stress 51
    Transcendental Meditation practice and anxiety 52

  Improved cardiovascular health..53
  Improved overall health 55
  Decreased medical expenses..56
  Younger biological age and longer life 57
  Conclusion...59

Chapter 6: Yoga and Dharma: Living Life in Accord with Nature's Design 60
  Dharma as natural law 61
  What does dharma mean in my life?..................................64
  Personal dharma 67
  Violation of natural law 69
  Is there scientific evidence? 70
  Improved moral decisions 72
  Reduced behavioral problems 74
  Results in prison rehabilitation programs 74
  Decreased cigarette, alcohol, and drug consumption 76
  Studies on collective consciousness 78

Chapter 7: The Fulfillment of Yoga in Higher States of Consciousness 79
  Established in Yoga perform action 80
  Seven states of consciousness 82
  The fourth state: Transcendental Consciousness 82
  The fifth state: Cosmic Consciousness 83
  The sixth state: God Consciousness 89
  The seventh state: Unity Consciousness 91
  Experiences of Unity Consciousness..................................93
  Experiences of Unity in the Upanishads 96

Chapter 8: The Transcendental Meditation-Sidhi Program...... 99
  Yogic Flying..100
  Experiences from the TM-Sidhi program 102
  Practical application of the TM-Sidhi program.............105

Chapter 9: Creating World Peace Through Yoga 107
    Collective consciousness 111
    The role of TM-Sidhi practice in creating world peace 112
    The future of world peace 117

Chapter 10: Misunderstandings About Yoga Philosophy 119
    Concentration 121
    Eliminating desires 124
    Remaining unattached 127
    Freedom from possessions 129
    Maintaining equanimity 131
    Renunciation..133
    Self-remembering 135
    Whose interpretation should I believe?...............................136
    Scientific research supporting Maharishi's interpretation 137

Chapter 11: Ashtanga Yoga: The Eight Limbs of Yoga 145
    Maharishi's commentary on the Patanjali Yoga Sutra 146
    The eight limbs of Yoga..147
    1. Yama 149
    2. Niyama..156
    3. Asana 162
    4. Pranayama 163
    5. Pratyahara 164
    6. Dharana 165
    7. Dhyan 166
    8. Samadhi..167

Chapter 12: Karma Yoga, Gyan Yoga, Bhakti Yoga, and Raja Yoga 169
    Karma Yoga 170
    Gyan Yoga 172
    Bhakti Yoga 174
    Raja Yoga..176

Chapter 13: Yoga in Human Physiology **177**
    Veda — the dynamic structure of pure consciousness..............177
    Veda in human physiology..182
    Structure and function of Veda and physiology......................182
    Yoga and the association fibers of the cerebral cortex 183

Chapter 14: Yoga and the Fulfillment of Life: Dharma, Artha, Kama, Moksha.. **187**
    Dharma..188
    Artha...189
    Kama...189
    Moksha 190
    Fulfillment 190

Summary and Conclusion **192**
    Regaining the lost knowledge of Yoga....................................194
    Our brain corresponds to the Yoga Sutra................................195

Additional Readings **196**
    Books 196
    Internet 196

References **197**

Index.. **217**

Introduction

Yoga is one of the fastest growing exercise and health trends in the world today. In the US alone Yoga studios are virtually everywhere: in malls, shopping centers, private homes, and office buildings. Articles and advertisements citing the benefits of Yoga regularly appear in both mainstream publications and new-age journals, and Internet sites provide everything from the do's and don'ts of Yoga practice to video demonstrations of difficult or obscure poses. Even in the sleepiest of small towns you can usually find a public class somewhere, while in more affluent communities concierge Yoga services provide the wealthy with tailor-made classes and private lessons in their homes.

Yoga accessories also play a role in what is now a multi-billion dollar industry. DVDs, special clothes, books, Yoga mats, and more are available on countless web sites, and rare is the department store or grocery without at least one shelf filled with Yoga products.

The reason for its immense popularity is simple: Yoga is good for you. Even though there are many different approaches, and despite the wide disparity in the skill level of its instructors, the results have, for the most part, been promising — Yoga keeps the body flexible and toned, can be helpful for reducing stress and tension, and may be useful for strengthening the heart and improving memory, concentration, and learning ability. Many Yoga teachers even promise relief from more serious health problems such as asthma, arthritis, chronic headaches, and hypertension, to name just a few. While the claims are many and the research still preliminary, Yoga practitioners have been enthusiastically vocal about their personal results and benefits.

Yoga is, however, much more than a popular exercise regime. Quietly waiting behind the generic term Yoga is a comprehensive philosophy and an array of techniques and procedures for unlocking the untapped potential that is said to be inside us all. According to the Yogis and seers of ancient India, each of us has infinite intelligence, creativity, and peace within, and we are all capable of enjoying a life of total freedom and fulfillment — and Yoga is prepared to give us the keys to unfold this hidden inner potential.

The notion that we have a vast storehouse of potential is not altogether surprising. There are descriptions of heightened levels of awareness and/or perception in the literature of most cultures. An example comes from the writing of John Addington Symonds, a 19th-century British poet and literary critic who described an experience of his transcendent self:

> It consisted in a gradual but swiftly progressive obliteration of space, time, sensation, and the multitudinous factors of experience which seem to qualify what we are pleased to call our Self. In proportion as these conditions of ordinary consciousness were subtracted, the sense of an underlying or essential consciousness acquired intensity. At last nothing

> remained but a pure, absolute, abstract Self. The universe became without form and void of content. But Self persisted, formidable in its vivid keenness.[1]

Such experiences have generally been limited, however, and rare has been the person who knew how to sustain them or recall them at will. Symonds himself noted that they diminished over time.

Many among the world community of Yoga practitioners are of course aware of the deeper implications of Yoga and enthusiastically seek the unfoldment of their inner potential. But the interpretations of Yoga philosophy are varied, and most modern approaches have proven arduous and often ineffective. To a certain extent, much of Yoga these days — at least with respect to this level of consideration — remains a speculative philosophy, without concrete, verifiable results.

Yoga practice can, however, unlock our inner self. Maharishi Mahesh Yogi, whose discussions on Yoga are the subject of this book, taught a holistic program that he brought to light from the ancient Vedic tradition of knowledge,* which includes a variety of approaches for refining and purifying mind, body, and environment. At the core of his programs lie the Transcendental Meditation® and TM-Sidhi® programs, whose origins are the ancient and authentic systems of Yoga meditation. These allow anyone to effortlessly dive within and experience the fountainhead of energy, creativity, and

---

* *Veda* means *knowledge*, and the Vedic tradition is the oldest continuous tradition of knowledge in the world. It includes an enormous literature as well as practical methods for developing higher states of consciousness.

intelligence deep inside, and to bring it out into life so that it can be lived and enjoyed.

In the following chapters we will examine Maharishi's programs and their scientific character, as well as their contributions to Yoga practice. We will also explore his lectures and writings on Yoga, paying close attention to a critical understanding: the distinction between the state of Yoga and Yoga practices. The state of Yoga is the experience of the inner self, the infinite reservoir of creativity and intelligence within each of us. Yoga practices are intended to help us gain that inner experience. Both are referred to in the ancient literature as Yoga, but many translators and scholars in recent centuries have confused the two, resulting in fundamental misconceptions about how to achieve the ultimate goal of Yoga practice — life in enlightenment.

In our final chapters, we will discuss the main types of Yoga, including *Karma Yoga*, *Gyan Yoga*, *Bhakti Yoga*, and *Ashtanga Yoga* in the light of Maharishi's commentaries. We'll begin with an illustrative story from the Bhagavad-Gita.

1
The State of Yoga

Arjuna's dilemma

The Bhagavad-Gita, often referred to simply as the *Gita*, is one of the most important and widely read texts on Yoga philosophy. It covers, in story form, the most significant themes and principles of Yoga, and when properly understood can be a practical guide for traversing the currents and pitfalls of modern life. It comprises a relatively small section of the great Sanskrit epic Mahabharat, which relates the events leading up to and following a battle between rival factions of a ruling family about 5,000 years ago.

The story begins as opposing armies gathered to embark upon what would become an eighteen-day ordeal to determine the rulership of the kingdom. As the conflict was set to commence, Arjuna, the hero, asked his charioteer to drive him between the armies so that he could survey them, determine his troops' readiness, and assess their prospects. Arjuna was considered the greatest warrior of his time, known throughout the land for his unparalleled proficiency in weaponry, his bravery and kindness, and his dedication to upholding the established principles of righteous behavior.

As he stood in his chariot observing the assembled armies, Arjuna became disheartened. He was a *kshatriya* — a member of society charged with the kingdom's administration and protection — and so his duty lay in conquering the enemy. The opposition, however, included many warriors and family members whom he considered dear, particularly his beloved elders and teachers. To kill his teachers and members of his family, regardless of their alliance with the opposition, was wrong and contrary to accepted conventions. His mind clearly understood the issues at hand, but his feelings were strong, and the thought of fighting against those he loved was breaking his heart. He expressed his concern to his charioteer and then threw down his bow and arrows, refusing to fight. He was overwhelmed with sorrow and his problem seemed insoluble.

Arjuna, however, was not speaking with a typical charioteer, for his driver was none other than Lord Krishna, famed throughout the Vedic literature* for his wisdom and enlightened teaching. Lord Krishna was the head of a large family participating in the conflict, and had been attempting for some time to avert the hostilities through personal diplomacy. He was unsuccessful, however, and was now faced

---

* The literature of the Vedic tradition includes several treatises on Yoga, the most important of which are the Yoga Sutra of Patanjali and the Bhagavad-Gita. We won't attempt to analyze these in great detail, but will instead examine some of the main principles from each in the light of Maharishi's commentaries, and in this way develop a broad and comprehensive vision of Yoga.

with a monumental calamity. Although his apparent role in the battle was to guide Arjuna's chariot and advise him about tactics, his more important function in the story was to explain the main tenets and principles of Yoga philosophy for the sake of Arjuna's growth and evolution.

Lord Krishna's reply to Arjuna's predicament has become the preeminent exposition of Yoga philosophy, remarkable for its simplicity and directness, along with its profound and practical insights. All other Yoga texts are elaborations upon the simple formula that Lord Krishna gave Arjuna in the moments before battle. And as we will see, his expressions reveal an approach to life that can help anyone, in any age, deal with their difficulties and make stronger, more positive, and more life-supporting decisions.

Lord Krishna's advice

Lord Krishna's response may seem surprising, at least for the modern reader. He initially ignored the question of Arjuna's participation in battle, instead guiding him toward a more comprehensive understanding of life and living. His intention was to disclose to Arjuna how he must organize himself for *any* event — how he should prepare to live his life, and thus deal more effectively with his immediate situation.

This was not what Arjuna was expecting, but he eagerly questioned Lord Krishna throughout their discourse, urging him into deeper explanations and greater elaborations upon the simple theme initially presented to him. The following excerpt encapsulates Lord Krishna's message to Arjuna:

त्रैगुरायविषया वेदा निस्त्रैगुरायो भवार्जुन
निर्द्वन्द्वो नित्यसत्त्वस्थो नियोंगक्षेम आत्मवान्

*Traigunyavishayā Vedā nistraigunyo bhavārjun
nirdwandwo nityasattwastho niryogakshema Ātmavān**
(Bhagavad-Gītā, 2.45)

...*Be without the three gunas, O Arjuna, freed from duality, ever firm in purity, independent of possessions, possessed of the Self.*[1]

Lord Krishna's admonition to *be without the three gunas* may seem obscure at first glance, but it is highly significant to our consideration of Yoga. In the Vedic understanding, the three *gunas* are the most fundamental forces in nature, responsible for everything that takes place in our lives and in our environment. Indeed, the whole universe is said to emerge from their interplay. *Be without the three gunas*, therefore, advises Arjuna to go beyond the material universe, to something that is more fundamental than even these most basic laws of nature.[2]

What can that possibly mean? How can one go beyond the material universe?

---

* The transliteration throughout this book is a simplified version of the standard convention used by academic texts. It is intended to give readers who do not have a Sanskrit background the opportunity to pronounce reasonably closely. For this reason it doesn't highlight some of the subtle distinctions usually found in Sanskrit transliteration.

Most modern commentators suggest that Lord Krishna wanted Arjuna to adjust his attitude — to become more dispassionate and feel less attached to the events and people around him. In this way he would not feel bound to the material world, and would (supposedly) feel better about entering into battle. But this is a critically wrong interpretation, which in Maharishi's view undermines the entire teaching of the Gita. For aren't you still very much within the influence of the three gunas when you create a mood of non-attachment? Aren't you still thinking thoughts and engaging in actions, and therefore still operating within the universe as we know it?

Furthermore, changing your attitude can be somewhat pointless, for it doesn't alter your nature or your current situation. Doing so would be roughly analogous to a poor person pretending to be rich: Regardless of attitude there would still be neither money nor purchasing power, and one might even be considered delusional. In the final analysis, there would be nothing to show for one's efforts other than a mood that probably won't last. And, as Maharishi points out, trying to create a mental state that is contrary to the realities of life is weakening to the mind and may cause a lack of integration.

So what was Lord Krishna advising Arjuna to do?

Maharishi's answer is central to his analysis of Yoga philosophy and provides a framework through which we can understand what Yoga is truly about. He explains that the most fundamental level of nature's functioning — beyond material structures and forms, beyond the three gunas — is an infinite field of pure intelligence.[3] In his *Science of Being and Art of Living*, published in 1963,[4] Maharishi describes this intelligence as *Being*, an unmanifest, unbounded, eternal, ocean of pure consciousness, pure wakefulness, which creates and administers everything, including what is seen and unseen throughout the universe. It created the far galaxies and governs their motion, and it created and administers the tiny molecules and subatomic particles that eternally move within every grain of creation. It never changes, and yet all the transformations we see around us take place within it. Maharishi describes Being as

> that one element in nature on the ground of which the infinite variety of creation is continuously emerging, growing, dissolving. The whole field of change emerges from this field of non-change, from this self–referral, immortal state of consciousness.[5]

Being is the source of creation and also its essential constituent, present in every particle. Every minute piece of creation is made of Being, as Maharishi explains:

> It is present in all forms, words, smells, tastes, and objects of touch. In all the objects of experience, in all the senses of perception and organs of action, in every phenomenon, in the doer and the work done, in all directions — north, south, east, and west — in all times — past, present, and future — It is uniformly present.[6]

Thus, when Lord Krishna recommended to Arjuna that he *be without the three gunas*, he wasn't suggesting a mood or philosophy — he was quite literally directing him toward this transcendental reality.

But how could Arjuna, on the verge of a monumental battle, locate this infinite intelligence, which is transcendental to everything we know? Was he to look around and see it? Or hear it? Or simply cling to a philosophy of understanding it as life's ultimate reality?

Fortunately, Being is easy to find, for it is not only the foundation of the material world, but also the source of our own individuality. It is our own intelligence deep within, the origin of our thoughts, ideas, creativity, intellectual analyses, and future plans — the creative intelligence that makes up our very nature and the source from which our individual life springs. Lord Krishna was therefore inviting Arjuna to go within and experience Being as the source of his own thought, his very essence.

The technique, as we will see in Chapter 2, is to take the awareness to quieter and quieter levels of the mind, to earlier stages in a thought's development, and then go beyond the thinking process to experience its origin. This source of thought is our own Self, our own inner nature, infinite, unbounded pure Being, the ultimate reality of ourselves and of the material universe. Only this level of life is truly beyond the three gunas. And, as Maharishi explains, it is not possible to experience it through the five senses:

> The transcendental state of Being lies beyond all seeing, hearing, touching, smelling, and tasting — beyond all thinking and beyond all feeling. This state of unmanifested, absolute pure consciousness of Being is the ultimate of life.[7]

Maharishi's point that it "lies beyond all seeing, hearing, touching, smelling, and tasting" is consistent with Lord Krishna's advice that Arjuna *be without the three gunas*. Clearly Lord Krishna is not suggesting that Arjuna create an attitude of non-attachment, but that he take his awareness deep within and experience Being as the foundational level of his own awareness.

When formulating a vocabulary to describe this transcendental reality, Maharishi settled upon a number of terms that help acquaint us with its characteristics. For example, *Being* describes it as a state of pure existence. *Pure consciousness* shows that it is consciousness without any kind of thought or idea — it is alone, by itself, pure wakefulness. Maharishi similarly referred to it as a state of *pure intelligence*, and also as *self-referral consciousness* — a continuum of awareness that is awake to itself, that knows itself alone with nothing outside it. And most important, it is the *Self*, because it is our inner nature.*

Likewise, Being is described in Sanskrit — the language of the Vedic literature — by many different words that also bring out its qualities. An example is *satchidananda*, which

---

* Maharishi often distinguished between two concepts of self: the individual, or small self (written with a small "s"), and the cosmic Self — Being, pure consciousness.

reveals that it is *sat* (absolute and unchanging, pure existence), *chit* (consciousness), and *ananda* (bliss).

There are also words to describe the experience of Being deep within as well as its significance to the experiencer. For example, the Sanskrit term *samadhi* means *the even state of the intellect*, the quietest level of our intelligence. *Turiya-chetana* — the fourth state of consciousness — provides us with an extremely important quality, for it reveals that the experience of Being is more than just a quiet level of the mind: It is a unique state that is different from waking, dreaming, and deep sleep — it is a fourth state of consciousness.

This description has been confirmed through repeated scientific experimentation, which has demonstrated that the experience of Being is both mentally and physiologically distinct: It is a unique fourth state, which Maharishi calls Transcendental Consciousness. We will discuss this more in Chapter 7, when we consider higher states of consciousness.

There is another highly important Sanskrit term for the inner experience of Being — *Yoga*. *Yoga* is derived from a Sanskrit verb meaning *to yoke* or *to join*, and is defined as the union, or joining, of individual awareness with its source, pure consciousness — infinite, unbounded, pure Being. This union of individual consciousness with Being is analogous to a wave settling down into the ocean. It may seem to have disappeared, but you can also say that it has become the whole ocean in all its greatness.[8] When our individual awareness quiets down and experiences Yoga, it is identifying itself with its own unbounded, blissful nature — it *is* that infinite Being.

This is one meaning of Yoga, but it doesn't mean that the postures we learn in a studio in Philadelphia are not Yoga — that is a different sense of the term, which we'll consider in the next chapter. We'll also see in Chapter 7 that the term *Yoga* includes the experience of higher states of consciousness, because in these our individual nature is also united with Being. For now, though, we'll focus our discussion on Yoga as the experience of the inner Self.

Freed from duality, ever firm in purity, and independent of possessions

The remainder of the above verse from the Bhagavad-Gita reveals much about the nature of Yoga. Lord Krishna tells Arjuna, for instance, that if he goes beyond the three gunas he will be *freed from duality*. Duality traditionally describes our relationship with the environment, because when engaged in sensory experience there are two fundamental components: ourself and the object of our experience. In other words, if you are looking at a rose, *you* are seeing the *rose*. This is the essence of duality.

The same is true whether you are sitting on a mountain viewing the scenery below, thinking quiet thoughts, or creating a mood of non-attachment — *you* are looking at the *scenery*, or *you* are thinking about *something*. Neither attitude nor philosophy can change this fundamental relationship between ourself and the environment around us.

So how can we be free from duality? Yoga is the experience of a state of unity, in the sense that one experiences the inner Self and nothing else — it is a state of pure subjectivity, pure wakefulness, with no thought or object of any kind. There is no other element of the experience other than our inner Self. We aren't experiencing the Self in the sense that it is an object — we *are* the inner Self. It may seem very abstract if you haven't had the experience, but when you do it seems most natural, most normal, for it is just yourself and yourself alone, a state of complete peace.

Lord Krishna also said that one who is beyond the three gunas is *ever firm in purity*, which describes a level of life that is beyond conflict, beyond mistakes, beyond every aspect of our infinite, ever-expanding universe. It is also *independent of possessions*, again referring to a state beyond the world of possessions and material objects. And finally Lord Krishna spoke of this state as *possessed of the Self*, referring to the experience of the inner Self, Transcendental Consciousness, the state of Yoga.

Commentators have long held that Lord Krishna was asking Arjuna to adjust his thinking, but as we can see these Sanskrit expressions do not describe a mere change of philosophy — they can only refer to the experience of Yoga, the transcendental state of consciousness.

The inner Self in the Upanishads

Throughout the literature of the Vedic tradition there are descriptions of the Self, of Yoga, and depictions of the unfoldment of life's full potential. One branch in particular, called Upanishad (or often "the Upanishads"), is well-known for its clear and descriptive accounts of the nature of pure consciousness and its experience within as the inner Self. Though the language of the individual Upanishads is stylistically different from modern English, it is clear that each portrays the same reality that Maharishi describes.

The Upanishads are often considered philosophical texts, in large part because the ability to regularly and systematically experience Yoga has been unavailable in modern times. But in reality they record the experiences of enlightened saints and sages of long ago.

The following selection informs us of several qualities of the experience of Yoga, while also advising us to experience it. The terminology used here for the inner Self is the Sanskrit *Atma*:

शिवं शान्तमद्वैतं चतुर्थं मन्यन्ते
स आत्मा स विज्ञेयः

Shivaṁ shāntam adwaitaṁ chaturthaṁ manyante sa Ātmā sa vigyeyaḥ
  (Nṛisiṁhottaratāpanīya Upanishad, 1)

The peaceful, the blissful, the undivided is thought to be the fourth; that is the Self, that is to be known.[9]

This verse tells us a great deal about the nature of our inner Self. It is peaceful — in fact it is a state of pure, infinite peace. It is blissful — its essential characteristic is bliss, complete fulfillment, total happiness. It is a fourth state of consciousness, Transcendental Consciousness. And it is our own Self, our own inner nature. *That is to be known* suggests that this level of awareness is not just theoretical — it is not the creation of ancient philosophers who pondered the mysteries of life and gave it their best guess — it is a concrete reality that can, and should, be experienced.

In the Gita, Lord Krishna didn't explain how to have this experience — at least it's not in the text — and so we are justified in wondering how we can follow his advice and experience Yoga. As it turns out, anyone can experience Yoga by using techniques that are part of the Yoga tradition. The texts themselves are not "how-to manuals," because learning the procedures for going within requires careful attention from a teacher trained to give the correct instruction at the proper time in order to accommodate the uniqueness of every student's nervous system and experience. For this reason, what Maharishi calls the "technologies of consciousness" are always taught in person, one-to-one, as they have been for millennia.

Lord Krishna and Arjuna conversed extensively throughout the Gita, culminating in Arjuna's final enlightenment in the final chapter. But the intervening sections of the discourse provide a thorough and complete discussion of Yoga, which we'll return to later. In the next chapter, we'll examine the Transcendental Meditation technique, which Maharishi taught around the world for over fifty years, and how it enables anyone to easily and effortlessly experience their inner Self, the infinite, eternal state of Yoga.

2
The Path of Yoga

Chapter 1 described Yoga as the union of individual awareness with its most fundamental nature, an infinite, eternal reservoir of pure consciousness, pure Being. This inner Self is an "ocean" of intelligence, existence, bliss, with neither beginning nor end, beyond time and space, and beyond all forms and phenomena.[1] It is the source of our thoughts, feelings, creativity, and ideas, and when we experience it deep within, we are enjoying the state of Yoga.

This description may appear somewhat speculative and philosophical, and indeed scholars and philosophers have regarded Yoga in this light for hundreds of years. But in reality the infinite bliss of Yoga is quite easy to experience, for there are techniques in the Yogic tradition that provide access to the inner Self. These have been passed down through the ages through a tradition of teachers.

These techniques, it turns out, are also called Yoga, which brings us to an interesting point of definition: Yoga is a state of consciousness — the experience of pure Being — as well as a path, or technique used to attain this experience. Thus there is a distinction between the *state of Yoga* and the so-called *path of Yoga*. This may seem a little confusing at first, but as we go forward we'll make clear which aspect of Yoga philosophy we are discussing.

The Yoga we usually encounter in the world, which involves various physical postures and breathing exercises, is part of the path of Yoga. When properly performed, these help refine the nervous system and remove impediments to the inner experience of the state of Yoga. The essence of Yoga practice, however, is meditation, in which one takes the awareness deep within — beyond thought, beyond the thinking mind, to the transcendental field of pure consciousness, the state of Yoga.

It is not the case, however, that all meditations allow us to experience Yoga. In fact most do not, for reasons we'll discuss shortly. But let's consider Maharishi's meditation, which allows us to easily and effortlessly experience the inner Self. Maharishi brought his meditation to light from the Vedic tradition and called it the Transcendental Meditation technique, because it allows us to go beyond — to transcend — thought, and experience the pure consciousness within.

Over the last fifty years scientists have subjected the Transcendental Meditation technique to extensive research, which has not only identified numerous physiological changes that accompany the experience of Yoga (such as unique brainwave patterns, changes in blood chemistry, etc.), but which has found this practice to be a most effective antidote to stress, fatigue, and even sickness and disease.

What is Transcendental Meditation practice?

The Transcendental Meditation (TM) technique is a simple, effortless, mental procedure that allows the awareness to settle to its quietest state — pure consciousness, Yoga. It is practiced for about 15 to 20 minutes twice a day, sitting comfortably with the eyes closed. It requires no system of belief, no philosophical or religious orientation, and it does not depend upon intellectual understanding or analysis. The technique is completely effortless, so much so that a ten-year-old child can effectively practice with as much success as an adult.

In the following excerpt, Maharishi describes his meditation while also providing an elegant description of Transcendental Consciousness, the state of Yoga:

> The Transcendental Meditation technique is an effortless procedure for allowing the excitations of the mind gradually to settle down until the least excited state of mind is reached. This is a state of inner wakefulness with no object of thought or perception, just pure consciousness aware of its own unbounded nature. It is wholeness, aware of itself, devoid of differences, beyond the division of subject and object — transcendental consciousness.[2]

When people learn to practice the Transcendental Meditation program they are often surprised at its naturalness and simplicity and how much is accomplished without effort or strain. While the ease of the practice has enabled millions of people worldwide to experience Yoga without hard work or arduous discipline, this quality is much more than a fortunate convenience — it is critical to the technique's effectiveness. Let's examine the mechanics of the Transcendental Meditation technique, and then in Chapter 3 we'll consider some experiences from practitioners as well as scientific research documenting its effects.

How the Transcendental Meditation program works

If you compare the human mind to a vast ocean, you may find a common element: Both have an active surface and silent depths. In this metaphor, the ocean's choppy waves are analogous to our thoughts, feelings, moods, and perceptions, and its quiet depths are like the silent pure consciousness deep within.[3] Generally we aren't aware of this silence, as we're engaged on the mind's surface — we go to work, sort through innumerable situations, go home, maybe watch a movie, almost always living in the active phases of life. This is like moving around among the waves of the ocean's surface, unaware of all that lies beneath.

During Transcendental Meditation practice, however, the mind turns within and begins to move toward progressively quieter levels. Ultimately it settles into the state of Yoga, its quietest state. Why? Because this meditation takes advantage of the mind's most fundamental tendency — to move in the direction of greater charm.

Given the opportunity, the mind will always seek more happiness and fulfillment. Ordinarily we may seek pleasure in greater success, more fun, or a more spacious home, but regardless of what we're doing the mind is always on the lookout for something more. For example, if you are sitting at home bored with some uninteresting task, your mind will spontaneously move toward anything in the environment that is more charming than the job at hand, whether a favorite song on the radio, an interesting conversation, or the thought of an old friend. It doesn't matter what the situation is, it is the nature of life to move in the direction of increasing happiness.

This is the tendency that the mind uses to locate and experience Yoga. Yoga is the most blissful, completely fulfilling state of life, and if given the chance the mind will always seek it. But in life we are generally directed outwards through the senses, and our awareness doesn't have the occasion to go within. Even when lost in quiet thought, the mind is still outward, swimming on its surface, so to speak. The Transcendental Meditation technique, however, provides the mind with an opportunity to remain lively and yet undirected, so that it can easily and effortlessly slip into its quietest and most enjoyable state — blissful pure consciousness, the state of Yoga. This is why Transcendental Meditation practice is effortless: We simply give the mind an opportunity to go within and it proceeds by itself, according to its own nature.

But what if you were to make some effort — if you were to concentrate, or try a little harder? Would you progress faster, or have longer and deeper meditations? Interestingly, you would make far less progress, because effort and concentration inhibit the ability to go within. The reason is simple: As it moves toward the silence of Yoga, the mind becomes increasingly quiet. The deeper you go during Transcendental Meditation practice, the more quiet the mind and body become. But if you concentrate or try to control the mind — even slightly — the effort creates mental activity, which will push the mind away from the silent depths. The result is that your awareness will automatically move back toward the surface.

This is an immense irony, because meditation is generally associated with concentration and contemplation, often involving great effort and discipline. A quick search of the Internet will reveal a multitude of meditation practices that suggest concentrating on a candle, controlling or removing thoughts and desires, imagining pleasant scenery, or trying to cultivate calmness and peace while pushing away thoughts and emotions that seem to be in the way. But as Maharishi so often pointed out, even a little effort is counterproductive because it keeps the mind active, engaged on the surface, and disallows the possibility of settling to quieter levels.

Aside from the Transcendental Meditation program, virtually all meditations require some kind of effort, either through concentration, control, or reflection, and though some may have value in a specific area — for example helping improve focus, or something like that — they do not promote the experience of Yoga, and in most cases they actually disallow it. In this sense they are not Yogic.

Some who are versed in the Yogic literature may take issue with this claim, for the texts are filled with references to vigorous concentration and the need for intense efforts to experience Yoga. Or so it may seem. In reality, interpretations that advocate effort and strain are based upon age-old misunderstandings, sometimes founded upon the mistranslation and misinterpretation of Sanskrit texts. And frequently they arise from confusion between the path of Yoga and the state of Yoga. We will examine Maharishi's discussion of this issue in Chapter 10.

Research comparing different meditations

According to Dr. Fred Travis, a widely published researcher on meditation and brain physiology, there are distinct patterns of brain functioning associated with different meditation practices.[4] In one study, Dr. Travis found that "focused attention" meditations — such as Tibetan Buddhist "loving kindness and compassion" practices, Zen and Diamond Way Buddhist techniques, and Chinese Qigong meditation — give rise to beta/gamma activity in the brain. Gamma waves are associated with a highly active brain, and therefore these meditations do not support the experience of quieter levels of the mind nor the peace and silence of Yoga.

Another category, known as "open monitoring," is a type of practice in which one attempts to remain cognizant of breath or thoughts. This group includes Buddhist Mindfulness and ZaZen, Chinese Qigong, and the meditations of the Sahaja Yoga tradition. These meditations produce theta waves as well as activity in the left frontal cortex, which is the part of the brain associated with evaluation. Such meditations have their own benefits and effects, but are also associated with more active brain physiologies, and thus do not bring one to the experience of Yoga. So far, the Transcendental Meditation program is the only meditation that produces the global coherent alpha waves that are associated with the experience of pure consciousness, the state of Yoga.

In addition, neural imaging during Transcendental Meditation practice shows that the front and back of the brain tend to be more awake and active than when one is just sitting with closed eyes, while the thalamus, the gateway of experience, is less active. This also supports the description of deep rest and increased alertness during meditation.

Next we will consider some experiences of Yoga, a few excerpts from the Vedic literature, and some additional research on the Transcendental Meditation program.

3
The Experience of Yoga

Maharishi's description of Yoga is logical and enticing, but those unfamiliar with his meditation may wonder whether he is formulating a speculative philosophy or whether there is something concrete, something real, that could be available to us all. This is an important question, for most of us are practical, and we like to spend our time on things with clearly definable and attainable results. And we may be less interested in ancient theories about what might or might not be a hidden reality somewhere deep inside.

To address this question, we'll now consider Yoga from three perspectives: historical records found in the Vedic literature, experiences from long-term practitioners of the Transcendental Meditation technique, and empirical research from the sciences. These will give us a better sense of whether Yoga is a living reality as opposed to a mystical philosophy, whether it is easily experienced, and whether it has practical value.

Experiences of pure consciousness in the Upanishads
The following is a small selection from the Upanishads, which contain descriptions of Yoga recorded long ago in ancient India. It will be interesting to compare these with

experiences from modern practitioners of the Transcendental Meditation program and then to consider them both in the light of scientific research.

एषा सर्वेषु भूतेषु गूढोत्मा न प्रकाशते

Eshā sarveshu bhūteshu gūdhotmā na prakāshate
(Katha Upanishad, 1.3.12)

The Self is hidden within all beings. It does not reveal itself.[1]

This first example makes a simple point: The Self, unbounded pure consciousness, is deep within everyone. It is hidden, not evident from the outside — it is transcendental. The Sanskrit term for the Self in this verse is Atma.

The next selection, from the Katha Upanishad, explains that the intelligence underlying the universe is also the inner Self.

पुरुषोऽन्तरात्मा सदा जनानां हृदये सन्निविष्टः

Purusho antarātmā sadā janānāṃ hṛidaye sannivishtaḥ
(Katha Upanishad, 2.3.17)

Purusha is the inner Self, ever established within the heart of everyone.[2]

Purusha is a Sanskrit term referring to the universal value of intelligence, pure Being.

The next selection cites some of the qualities and characteristics of the inner Self. We see here that it is peaceful, effulgent, pure intelligence. And because it is transcendental, it is beyond the ups and downs of relative life, and therefore unswayable, unwavering — unshakable. On that level there is only the inner Self, so there is nothing to threaten it or obstruct it in any way — it is beyond any feeling of fear.

सुप्रशान्तः सकृज्ज्योतिः समाधिरचलोऽभयः

Suprashāntaḥ sakṛijjyotiḥ samādhir achalo 'bhayaḥ
(Māndukya Upanishad, 3.37)

[The Self is] deeply peaceful, eternally effulgent, the state of even intelligence, unshakable, and without fear.[3]

We discussed the following in Chapter 1, but it is worth mentioning again, as it provides several qualities of the inner Self while also emphasizing its availability for human experience. The Self, Atma, is described as peaceful, blissful, a state of unity, and the fourth state of consciousness (distinct from waking, dreaming, and sleeping). And most significantly, *it is to be known* — it can, and should, be experienced.

शिवं शान्तमद्वैतं चतुर्थं मन्यन्ते स आत्मा स विज्ञेयः

Shivaṁ shāntam adwaitaṁ chaturthaṁ manyante sa Ātmā sa vigyeyaḥ
(Nṛisiṁhottaratāpanīya Upanishad, 1)

The peaceful, the blissful, the undivided is thought to be the fourth; that is the Self, that is to be known.[4]

But the question still stands: Can we really experience it? Is it truly available to everyone? Is it not unreasonable to suspect that these verses are merely the remnant of an ancient philosophy?

Experiences of Yoga are not only common among practitioners of the Transcendental Meditation technique, they are very much the rule, though the clarity may vary due to the amount of stress in the nervous system. Below are a few experiences from advanced practitioners, most of whom have been meditating twice a day for many years. While beginning students generally have very deep experiences of the inner Self right from the start, the clarity we will see in the following often takes some time to develop. Note how the qualities of Yoga mentioned in the Upanishads are found in these experiences.[5] (Each of the following paragraphs is a separate experience.)

> During the Transcendental Meditation program my awareness expanded in a very satisfying fullness. I sensed the bliss of silent Being [pure consciousness, Yoga]. Then I saw that bliss was moving outward — blissful waves emerging from inner silence and processing into the manifested reality. Radiating out from my Being over and over again, the waves were becoming manifest. The fullness I was experiencing was made up of those waves radiating in every direction, and becoming everything around me.

> During [Transcendental Meditation practice] I slide immediately into Being. It is completely effortless. The experience of silence is completely full. There are no fluctuations and the breath is very still while I float in this infinite bliss of Being. And there comes a thought that I could never leave or would never want to leave this total fullness of silence.

> Seated in a deep, unified state of motionless bliss, Self established in Itself, I feel deeply fulfilled, beyond the need or thought of anything. Even though this state is a field of nothingness, it is also a self-sufficient field that has everything in it, whole and complete.
>
> I experience an ongoing expansion of my small self awareness into the eternal unbounded ocean of infinity, which is simply and profoundly bliss; the ever-increasing levels and waves of realizations continue to unfold every moment.
>
> Meditation was filled with light and bliss; I experienced pure consciousness as an unbounded and synchronous continuum, infinite connectedness, and in this state I was all that is. I felt the whole universe was my Self. I was on the royal road of existence where one does nothing and accomplishes everything.[6]
>
> Boundless infinitude, beautiful bliss, total silence. In activity a powerful silent wholeness rests on the surface of everything. A beautiful softness connects and interfuses all I see.[7]

The last one includes experiences both during and after the practice, revealing how pure consciousness begins to become part of daily life even in the midst of the most dynamic activity. This will be the topic of our next chapter, which considers the development of our mental potential — what happens as the benefits of Transcendental Meditation practice accumulate.

Research on Transcendental Meditation practice

The experiences above are compelling, but one might still wonder if they are real, or whether they were created by a mood or wishful thinking, or perhaps imagined after reading descriptions in the Upanishads. It is a reasonable question, and most critical readers will want more evidence. Even though such experiences are commonplace among Transcendental Meditation practitioners, there is nothing quite so convincing as empirical data.

The body of scientific research on Maharishi's programs is impressive, both in quantity and quality. To date there have been over 350 peer-reviewed studies, conducted at top educational and research institutions around the world and published in academic and scientific journals. Let's look at a few that support the subjective experiences of Yoga. In later chapters we will examine others as appropriate to the topic.

A state of deep rest

During Transcendental Meditation practice the mind settles to progressively more refined levels of thinking, until it passes beyond thought and arrives at its source: pure, unbounded, infinite consciousness, Transcendental Consciousness, the state of Yoga. As the mind settles to the silence of Yoga, the body also becomes increasingly quiet, enjoying a deep state of rest. This rest is especially effective for releasing stress that has accumulated in the physiology (see Chapter 5).*

---

* Scientists and researchers define stress differently, but in this context it refers to a physiological abnormality in the nervous system that is caused by overload. A hectic day, an altercation with a friend, pressure at work, or even an overpoweringly happy experience — these are all common circumstances that can produce stress in the physiology.

Scientists have described Transcendental Consciousness as a wakeful hypometabolic state, which in lay terms means *restful alertness* — the body rests deeply while the mind is fully awake. It is a unique state, physiologically distinct from waking, dreaming, and deep sleep. This is an important point, because it corroborates the verse from the Upanishads that describes the experience of the inner Self as a fourth state of consciousness.

Scientists assess rest during Transcendental Meditation practice in a variety of ways. One method is to measure the amount of oxygen intake: When we are active we breathe more, and when we rest we breathe less. Researchers have found that there is a significant reduction of oxygen intake during Transcendental Meditation practice, indicating a state of deep rest.[8]

Galvanic skin response (GSR), skin conductance, is an electrophysiological measure of calmness or restfulness. When we are more active, there is an increase in skin moisture, whereas a more restful state results in less moisture and therefore lower skin conductivity. Researchers have found significantly reduced basal skin conductance during Transcendental Meditation practice, again indicating an extremely deep state of rest.[9]

Another indicator of physiological rest is the level of lactate in the blood. When we exercise, blood lactate tends to increase, and when we are resting and relaxing, levels tend to recede. High levels of lactate have also been associated with anxiety and high blood pressure. Studies have found that Transcendental Meditation practice produces significantly decreased levels of blood lactate, in comparison to controls.[10]

These studies are important, but there is even stronger evidence. Using a sophisticated statistical tool known as meta-analysis, which combines the conclusions of related experiments, researchers examined thirty-two studies that employed the three measures cited above — basal skin conductance, respiration rate, and plasma level. Their conclusions corroborated and strengthened the original findings that Transcendental Meditation practice produces a profound and unique state of physiological rest.[11]

Increased wakefulness and a more orderly brain
Along with deep rest, practitioners report a state of heightened wakefulness. This has been corroborated in many studies by measuring electroencephalographic (EEG) patterns. Researchers have found that during Transcendental Meditation practice there is an increase in regularity and intensity of EEG alpha activity, which is generally associated with restful alertness, creativity, and reduced anxiety and stress.[12]

In addition, Transcendental Meditation practice results in greater orderliness of brain function, as measured by increased EEG coherence between and within the brain hemispheres.[13] This means that if you measure the electrical output from different parts of the brain during Transcendental

Meditation practice, you'll find that the brainwaves tend to "fall into phase" with each other — they become more similar in appearance. This correlation among brainwaves is called EEG coherence. Increased EEG coherence is initially found during meditation, but soon becomes evident afterwards, in activity. This is an indication that the experience of Yoga — the experience of the inner wakefulness of pure consciousness — is growing in life.

Scientists believe that an increase in brainwave coherence indicates a better working relationship among the different parts of the brain, resulting in greater mental and physiological efficiency. Indeed, research has found that high levels of EEG coherence during Transcendental Meditation practice are associated with higher creativity, greater efficiency in learning new concepts, more principled moral reasoning, higher verbal intelligence, less neuroticism, higher academic achievement, and greater neurological efficiency (faster spinal reflex recovery). They are also associated with clearer experiences of Yoga.[14]

In an especially important study, scientists found increased global EEG coherence during Transcendental Meditation practice in all brainwave frequencies (theta, slow alpha, and fast alpha) and all pairs of electrodes (six pairs were placed in the frontal-central area). Subjects who had been randomly assigned to a control technique showed no significant change.[15] This increase of EEG coherence indicates a more orderly, coherent style of brain functioning.

Periods of natural respiratory suspension

The Vedic literature is filled with stories of great Yogis sitting deep in meditation without breathing. Modern practitioners of the Transcendental Meditation technique report that it is indeed a quiet state, in which they experience the deep silence of pure consciousness along with minimal activity of mind and body. But could one actually stop breathing?

Scientific research confirms that during extended experience of Transcendental Consciousness, respiration ceases for brief periods. This does not, of course, mean that the meditator is oxygen-deprived, but rather that the physiology is resting so deeply that the need for oxygen is significantly reduced.

In one study, researchers found that during longer experiences of pure consciousness individuals not only displayed a suspension of respiration, but also higher mean EEG coherence over all frequencies and brain areas, in contrast to control periods in which subjects voluntarily held their breath.[16] This finding is especially important as it shows that the state of Yoga is real and not a product of mood, imagination, or philosophical belief. And the increased EEG coherence further demonstrates that this experience of Yoga is highly orderly, apparently more so than normal waking consciousness.

Frequency of pure consciousness experiences

A study of 140 students practicing the Transcendental Meditation technique found a significant increase in frequency of experience of pure consciousness throughout their undergraduate years. Frequency of experience correlated with results of a Constructive Thinking Inventory (CTI) including Global Constructive Thinking, Emotional Coping, and Behavioral Coping.[17] CTI is a standardized test of practical or experiential intelligence, which is the ability to understand and deal with the everyday environment — to act appropriately, say the right thing, or apply life's lessons at the right time. Practical intelligence is often considered a better predictor of success in life than other intelligence measures, such as IQ.

The same study also found a significant increase in ego (self) development as a result of Transcendental Meditation practice. Improvement in ego development measures the emergence and development of our sense of self. As our own ego grows and matures, we develop the ability to better interpret the world around us and interact more appropriately. Improvements in ego development thus contribute directly to our quality of life.

In addition, the researcher matched students' descriptions of their experiences with principles of Yoga found in the traditional Yoga texts, demonstrating that higher states of consciousness (see Chapter 7) as presented in these ancient texts is available to contemporary undergraduate students.[18]

In this chapter we have examined the experience of Yoga from three perspectives: the Upanishads from the Vedic literature, experiences from practitioners of the Transcendental

Meditation program, and also empirical research. Taken together, these support the view that the state of Yoga is physiologically and experientially unique, and that practitioners of the Transcendental Meditation program are experiencing the same level of awareness described historically in the Upanishads. In the next chapter we will look at how the daily experience of Yoga enables us to unfold our mental potential.

4
Yoga and the Development of Mental Potential

Every school, every university — every educational institution of any kind — has a common aspiration: to develop the full potential of its students. They may differ about what constitutes "full potential," and even the teachers within a school may not always agree, but the universal sentiment is that all young people — and indeed every adult — should develop their latent potential in order to increase the likelihood of a richer, more enjoyable, more productive life.

Educational institutions are not alone in advocating the need for the realization of human potential. Since the 1960s the interest in human development has increased exponentially. Today there are innumerable philosophies and self-help programs that attempt to uncover untapped athletic prowess, interpersonal skills, career competence, and even hidden reserves of brain power. The common thread among them all is the universal sentiment that we can do more, be more, and live a more fulfilled life.

The desire for uncovering hidden potential lies at the heart of Yoga's recent surge in popularity, for Yoga philosophy holds that each of us has infinite creativity, intelligence, and bliss within. This hidden potential, according to the ancient Yoga texts, can be directly experienced and awakened in our life. To this end there is a variety of Yoga programs, including physical exercises (*asanas*), dietary and purification programs (*Ayur-Veda**), and meditation for the development of higher levels of consciousness.

The benefits of Transcendental Meditation practice are both immediate and cumulative, and point to the rapid unfoldment of our mental potential. From the earliest days practitioners begin developing their creativity and intelligence, on the basis of a more efficiently functioning brain and nervous system.

The human brain

The brain is an extraordinarily sophisticated organ. It performs innumerable activities, often simultaneously, enabling us to love, remember, solve difficult problems, and plan for the future, while also controlling ongoing physiological functions that are essential to our life and wellbeing. Even as we ponder the solution to a complicated problem, the brain

---

* Ayur-Veda is the world's oldest continuously practiced tradition of medicine, recognized by the World Health Organization (WHO) as a valid system of natural health care. While it effectively treats disease, it emphasizes prevention through enlivening the body's own intelligence. Maharishi integrated the traditional principles of Ayur-Veda with the knowledge and technologies for the development of consciousness, a critical connection that had been lost in recent centuries. The resulting system is known as Maharishi Ayur-Veda® to distinguish it from the practices currently found in India, which seldom take into account the growth and development of consciousness.

is monitoring the body's organs and systems through an intricate network of chemical and nerve messengers, dispatching commands that regulate body temperature, breathing, balance, etc. At the same time it is supervising our defenses against harmful invaders, such as bacterial or viral infections. If we contract the flu, it activates processes within the immune system to destroy it.

With so many complex tasks to perform, the brain's ability to interact quickly and appropriately with its different parts, as well as with the various systems throughout the body, is critical. Just imagine the mechanisms your brain administers while you play a friendly game of tennis. It will oversee your response to your opponent's serve by directing myriad precise muscle movements in the legs, arm, hands, etc., while also monitoring and addressing physiological processes such as blood pressure, heart rate, breathing, and body temperature. And it may also be recollecting your opponent's tactical tendencies and formulating an appropriate response.

All of this and much more takes place in tiny fractions of a second. If all these functions are well integrated, you may act quickly and appropriately, but slight hesitations or impediments in the coordination between different parts of the brain and the nervous system may result in mental and physical errors.

This example illustrates a brain that must work quite efficiently, but the principle holds true no matter what you do. You may not be a tennis player — you may not even have a fast-paced life — but your mental and physical wellbeing nonetheless depend upon a high level of neurophysiological efficiency.

Research on the Transcendental Meditation program and mental potential

Among the many physiological changes that take place during Transcendental Meditation practice, perhaps the most intriguing is the increase in global coherent alpha waves associated with the experience of Yoga. Brain wave coherence, as we've seen, indicates a greater coordination between the brain's parts as well as more orderly functioning of the prefrontal cortex. Significantly, as one continues with the practice this coherence becomes increasingly apparent outside of meditation, and as a result practitioners become more integrated, resourceful, mentally flexible, and adaptable.

This is a key finding, for positive change during the practice alone is not enough to justify spending time in meditation. It may be somewhat satisfying to know that our brain is exhibiting higher coherence between and within its different quadrants during meditation, but our main objective is to see growth afterwards — changes that will make us feel better and perform more effectively. In the following section we will see how improved brain functioning through the Transcendental Meditation technique results in a wide range of benefits such as growth of intelligence and higher achievement at work and in school.

Growth of intelligence

Years ago, IQ tests were the primary measure of intelligence. You were considered intelligent if you had a high IQ, whereas a low IQ was thought to indicate less intelligence. Over time, however, researchers realized that IQ measurement is inadequate — that a high IQ doesn't necessarily predict success, and many with lower IQs are more productive, happy, and better able to fulfill their dreams.

It seems that IQ measures certain types of intelligence but doesn't account for others. For example, it doesn't measure creativity, emotional intelligence, or our ability to act appropriately and practically. Thus, even though studies have shown that the IQ of practitioners of the Transcendental Meditation technique increases even after adolescence[1] — a noteworthy finding in its own right — this does not by itself indicate holistic growth of intelligence.

Recent research, however, indicates that intelligence develops holistically from Transcendental Meditation practice. In one study, a scientist in Taiwan used seven standardized tests to measure an array of cognitive, emotional, and perceptual functions of 362 meditating students. Even though the students had only been practicing the Transcendental Meditation technique for six months, they showed improvements in five different measures: *practical intelligence, creativity, field independence, mental efficiency,* and *fluid intelligence.*[2]

These types of intelligence represent different ways in which we interact with the world. For example, we may need to come up with a new idea, or we may want to apply something we already know in a unique way. This kind of challenge requires us to use our *creativity*. Creativity is not the sole province of artists and musicians — everyone uses it to some degree — but we also have the potential for infinite creativity, which we can access.

In this study, the researcher found that the Chinese students did in fact grow in creativity as a result of their Transcendental Meditation practice. He used a test that measures whole brain creativity, which requires a balanced use of intellect and feelings. The test results indicated a significant increase in the creativity of the meditating students compared to non-meditating controls.

Sometimes we just need to be practical, and know how to act appropriately — how to say or do the right thing at the right time. Psychologists call this *practical intelligence*. Interestingly, practical intelligence is generally a better predictor of success in both career and relationships than IQ.

In this study the researcher used a test that measures changes in mental outlook as well as practical abilities such as the capacity to work with others. It also predicts success in work and social relationships. The meditating group improved significantly in practical intelligence when compared to the non-meditating controls.

Field-independent people are more prone to disregard irrelevant elements of a situation and focus upon what is useful — they are better able to comprehend more broadly and see the big picture while attending to details. Someone with less field independence, on the other hand, may tend to be distracted by what is irrelevant. A field-independent person is also more likely to be receptive to other people's opinions and perspectives and less likely to be unduly influenced by peers. This study documented significant growth in field independence among the meditating group as compared to the controls.

An important aspect of the ability to interact with the environment is our *mental efficiency*. When the need arises, can we recall necessary information and quickly distinguish between what is relevant and irrelevant? Can we process large amounts of data and quickly come up with an effective solution? This is an extremely important part of holistic brain development, because it measures the degree to which the different parts of the brain work together.

This study examined the rate of taking in and measuring simple stimulus information. The improvements among the meditating students when compared to controls indicate a growth of alertness and ability to focus, both of which are critical for learning.

In a separate study also measuring mental efficiency, university students practicing the Transcendental Meditation program showed improved clustering in short-term memory after forty days of practice as well as faster solution of arithmetic problems, indicating increased organization and efficiency of the thinking process.[3]

An additional study on cadets at a military academy in Brazil who were practicing the Transcendental Meditation technique also indicated greater mental efficiency by demonstrating improved cognitive performance, as measured by increased speed during a task of concentrated attention and improved memory of details.[4]

Fluid intelligence is the capacity to think logically and solve problems in new situations, independently of previously held knowledge. In other words, a person with a high level of fluid intelligence is better able to identify patterns and relationships underlying different situations in order to logically solve problems. The study on the Taiwanese students found significant improvements in fluid intelligence among the Transcendental Meditation practitioners.

In theory, growth of intelligence should translate into greater success, whether academic, professional, or in our everyday life. The following are a few studies indicating improved academic achievement among students practicing the Transcendental Meditation program:

- Elementary school children showed significant gains on a nationally standardized test of basic skills, within just one school year of learning.[5]

- Research has also shown that students practicing the Transcendental Meditation technique are more creative, receive better grades, and make better decisions.[6]

- University students also improved their academic performance after learning the Transcendental Meditation technique, in one study showing a significant increase in grade point average over the three grading periods following their instruction, while control students remained at about the same level.[7]

- Engineering students in the UK pursuing their master's degrees showed improved performance on their standard examinations after six months of Transcendental Meditation practice, compared with randomly assigned control students from the same academic program.[8]

The brain is not the only part of human physiology to benefit. Indeed, Transcendental Meditation practice profoundly affects every part of the physiology, leading to the reduction of stress and improvements in health. This is the topic of our next chapter.

5
Yoga and Health

Every day millions of people throughout the world practice Yogic postures and positions in studios or in the comfort of their homes. Why? For the most part to improve their health. Experts claim a variety of health benefits from Yoga exercise (*Hatha Yoga*), and many Yoga practitioners agree.

But what about the health benefits from experiencing the *state* of Yoga? And from the *practice* of Yoga meditation? In this chapter we will examine a sample from the hundreds of scientific studies on Transcendental Meditation practice to illustrate its influence on health.

Stress

It's difficult to discuss health without considering stress. Stress has become endemic in modern societies and is increasingly recognized as a factor in many of our most serious health concerns. Everyone is familiar with stressful situations — a bad day at work or school, an argument with a friend or colleague, financial or work-related pressures, etc. — but apparently these have a residual effect, a structural or material abnormality that accumulates over time and impedes the smooth operation of our physiology. That accumulation is what we mean here by stress.

Chronic stress disrupts the functioning of almost every bodily system. It can contribute to high blood pressure, stroke, heart attack, atherosclerosis, and coronary artery disease, as well as anxiety, diabetes, and asthma. It is also known to suppress the immune system, leaving us vulnerable to a wide variety of afflictions.

Almost half of adults suffer from stress-related disease, and 75% – 90% of all doctors' office visits are for stress-related ailments and complaints. In fact medical experts believe that up to 90% of disease is caused or complicated by stress. The Occupational Safety and Health Administration (OSHA) in the US has recently reported that stress costs American industry more than $300 billion annually.

Among the most serious consequences of stress is its impact on brain functioning. Stressful situations activate hormones that repress the higher brain, including the so-called executive functions that control planning, abstract thinking, initiating and completing tasks, moral reasoning, and adaptation to changing circumstances. Inhibiting these functions can be harmful in any situation, but it is especially problematic for the young, for whom there is a serious potential for permanently interrupting brain development.

Stress in students' lives

Students today cope with an increasingly complex society with difficulties unknown to previous generations. They must handle rigorous academics and the pressures of college entry or career planning, plus a broad array of social challenges, such as higher rates of broken or dysfunctional families, drug and alcohol abuse, school violence, and a growing atmosphere of fear in their schools.

These pressures come at a time when children's brains are undergoing delicate stages of development. Between birth and age twenty, neural connections form that influence how they behave and respond to the environment, and once this development is complete it can be extremely difficult to change.

Disrupting development can cause long-lasting harm with severe behavioral implications. Excess stress during the development of neural networks can result in permanent "wiring" to stressful reactions, resulting in long-term tendencies to overreact in non-stressful situations. Prolonged stress can also result in learning difficulties and permanent damage to brain development.

A recent study found that verbal abuse from peers, bullying, can create abnormalities in the corpus callosum, a bundle of neural fibers that connect the left and right cerebral hemispheres.[1] These fibers aid communication between the cerebral hemispheres and also carry neural traffic to and from the cerebral cortex and other parts of the brain. Damage to the corpus callosum disrupts information flow, resulting in, among other things, a diminished capacity to make moral judgments. A child or adult with difficulty making proper moral decisions may become susceptible to inappropriate and even criminal behavior.

Researchers have also found that prolonged stress kills brain cells, and harms memory and other basic mental functions.[2] As a result, children under continued stress become predisposed to long-term mental health problems, such as depression, anxiety, and drug and alcohol abuse. Research has shown that adolescents are twice as likely to drink and take drugs when they are under stress.

Transcendental Meditation practice and stress
It isn't always possible to eliminate a stressful environment. We tend to live active lives, engaged in dynamic lifestyles that are necessary for our progress and comfort, and stress seems to be an inevitable part of the modern landscape. What we can do, however, is remove accumulated stress from the body and create a stronger nervous system that is resilient to the harmful effects of stressful situations.

Transcendental Meditation practice creates a unique physiological state in which the body rests deeply while the mind enjoys a quiet level of increased alertness. During this state, the body takes the opportunity to correct and repair its functioning: It releases accumulated stress and fatigue, and rejuvenates itself, so that at the end of meditation we feel fresh and rested, even following a long, busy day at work. Regular practice also cultures the nervous system to increasingly sustain both silence and activity simultaneously — we begin to experience the quietness of Transcendental Consciousness even in the midst of dynamic activity. This growth of silence enables us to endure the ups and downs of life from a growing platform of calmness, so that even a bad day or a difficult interaction creates far less residual stress in the nervous system. The circumstances may continue — you might be in a hurry for a job interview and find yourself blocked by a major traffic jam — but your mind remains more calm and your body does not accumulate so much stress.

Anxiety and stress often go hand-in-hand. Anxiety can arise from stressful circumstances, but it is also a major cause of stress. We can reduce stress by containing anxiety, but it is extremely difficult to do so by force of will. Research on Transcendental Meditation practice, however, clearly demonstrates its effectiveness for spontaneously reducing anxiety; practitioners become significantly less anxious without even thinking about it — they naturally find themselves more cool, calm, and peaceful, and better able to deal with stressful situations without incurring stress.

Transcendental Meditation practice and anxiety
We saw earlier that different types of meditation have different results. One feature of Transcendental Meditation practice is that it has a significantly more profound impact on anxiety than other meditations. In a meta-analysis examining 146 studies on meditation and anxiety, researchers found that Transcendental Meditation practice is significantly more effective in reducing trait anxiety than meditations using concentration, contemplation, or other techniques.[3]

Researchers have also found significant reductions in anxiety in other contexts. A study in the US automobile industry, for example, found that executives and workers showed markedly decreased anxiety after just three months of Transcendental Meditation practice,[4] as did Japanese industrial workers after five months of practice.[5] Another study found that young people who had been referred to juvenile court for legal offenses exhibited marked reductions in anxiety after taking a Transcendental Meditation course.[6]

Perhaps no environment produces as much anxiety and stress as a maximum security prison, and yet prisoners who learned the Transcendental Meditation program showed significantly decreased levels of trait (general) anxiety.[7] And of particular interest to special-needs educators, students with a current diagnosis of attention deficit hyperactivity disorder (ADHD) who learned the Transcendental Meditation technique displayed reduced stress, anxiety, and ADHD symptoms after just three months of practice.[8]

Improved cardiovascular health

According to the World Health Organization (WHO), more people die from cardiovascular disease each year than from any other cause.[9] The current WHO estimate is 17 million deaths per year, which is expected to rise to 23.6 million per year by 2030. In the US, heart disease is the number one killer, accounting for 25% of deaths annually.[10] Stress, cholesterol, and high blood pressure are among its principal risk factors, and lifestyle choices such as cigarette and alcohol use can further exacerbate its onset.

Over the last 20 years, the National Institutes of Health (NIH) in the US has granted more than $25 million to research investigating the effectiveness of the Transcendental Meditation program in counteracting cardiovascular disease. The individual studies were conducted at leading universities throughout the US. Below are some of the results.

A 2007 meta-analysis analyzed 107 studies on the effects of various meditation practices on stress reduction and blood pressure. The study found that only the Transcendental Meditation program has a statistically significant impact on reducing high blood pressure among hypertensive subjects.[11]

In another meta-analysis, this time on both systolic and diastolic blood pressure, researchers examined all published randomized, controlled clinical trials that measured the effects of the Transcendental Meditation program on blood pressure. This included nine studies with a total of 711 subjects. Transcendental Meditation practice was found to have a significant effect on reducing both systolic and diastolic blood pressure.[12]

A number of other studies have further documented the effects of Transcendental Meditation practice on cardiovascular disease. In the following findings, the beneficial results arose only from the meditation practice — diet and exercise were sometimes used by the control groups, but the

Transcendental Meditation program was responsible for the results:

- Decreased systolic blood pressure among cardiac heart disease patients[13]
- Improved quality of life for congestive heart failure patients[14]
- Reduced blood pressure in at-risk teens[15]
- Reduced atherosclerosis[16]
- Reduced insulin resistance among cardiac disease patients[17]
- Regression of atherosclerosis[18]
- Reduced blood pressure and use of hypertensive medication[19]
- Reduced metabolic syndrome[20]
- Relaxation of blood vessels[21]
- Enhanced longevity[22]
- Reduced cholesterol among subjects with documented high cholesterol (there were no changes in diet)[23]

Improved overall health

When we rid ourselves of stress, a natural result is improved health. Even if we don't have specific stress-related complaints, stress has a damaging effect on the entire body, including the immune system.

A number of studies have shown that Transcendental Meditation practice produces significantly improved overall health. For example, a study in Cambodia found that university students improved in general health after three months of Transcendental Meditation practice, in contrast to non-meditating students from two other universities.[24]

In another study, executives and employees in the US automotive industry who had been practicing the Transcendental Meditation program for three months reported fewer physical and mental health complaints, in comparison to controls from the same work site.[25] Industrial workers in Japan also had fewer physical complaints after five months of practice, in comparison to workers in a control group.[26]

Decreased medical expenses
One of the most efficient ways of studying the effects of a health-promoting program is to measure cost savings in a publicly-funded healthcare system. A number of studies on Canadian citizens have found that Transcendental Meditation practice significantly diminishes health-related problems, as evidenced by reduced visits to the doctor and fewer hospital outpatient visits.

A study in Quebec, for example, compared data from 1,418 people who had taken the Transcendental Meditation course with 1,418 controls randomly selected from individuals of the same age, gender, and region. The researchers then compared the two groups, measuring the annual percentage change in inflation-adjusted government payments for physicians' services over fourteen years. Before the Transcendental Meditation course, there was no significant difference between the two groups, but the subjects who learned showed an annual decline of 13.8% in payments for physicians' services.[27] In other words, the health of the meditators improved significantly relative to the controls.

Another study, this time utilizing five years of medical insurance data from approximately two thousand Transcendental Meditation practitioners, found significantly less hospitalization and significantly fewer outpatient doctor visits for both medical and surgical procedures, in comparison to the average of all other insured persons.[28] A separate study found that those who participated in Maharishi's programs, including the Transcendental Meditation technique, showed greatly reduced hospital stays, outpatient hospital visits, and overall medical expenditures in comparison to norms.[29]

Younger biological age and longer life

If your aunt says that she is 60 years old, she is referring to her "chronological age." But there is a different measure called "biological age," which pertains to the body's state when compared to population norms — someone could be 60 years old chronologically but have the physiology of a 42-year-old. This would be highly desirable, of course, as a younger biological age bears the promise of a longer, more productive, and potentially happier life. In determining biological age a researcher generally considers factors such as brain response to stimuli, changes in the body's physical structure, sensory awareness, and motor skill performance.

Researchers have found that practitioners of the Transcendental Meditation program have significantly lower biological ages than their chronological ages. In one study, researchers found that the meditators had a lower biological age when compared to a control group, and also that length of time practicing was positively correlated to the disparity between these two measure of age.[30]

Researchers have also found that Transcendental Meditation practitioners show higher levels of plasma dehydroepiandrosterone sulfate (DHEA-S) than controls. DHEA-S is a hormone involved in our response to stress, which usually declines with age after the mid-twenties. Higher levels later in life are associated with better health.[31]

An expected outcome of a younger biological age is a longer, healthier life. You might anticipate this from a program that significantly decreases stress, and indeed empirical research strongly supports the prediction. In a follow-up study of elderly people (average age 80.7 years) who had been randomly assigned to either Transcendental Meditation instruction or to one of three control groups, those who took the Transcendental Meditation course showed a significant increase in longevity when compared to the other three groups.[32]

In another study — a long-term, randomized trial — researchers studied the death rates of 202 men and women (average age 71) who had mildly elevated blood pressure. The study tracked the subjects for up to eighteen years, and found that those practicing the Transcendental Meditation technique showed a 23% decrease in mortality due to all causes, and a 30% decrease in the rate of cardiovascular mortality, in comparison to controls. The control group participated in techniques such as mindfulness or progressive muscle relaxation, or took part in health education.[33]

Conclusion

In this chapter we have considered a sample of the scientific research on health benefits from Transcendental Meditation practice. We have seen that the deep rest associated with the practice allows the physiology to refresh and rejuvenate itself, and dissolve deeply rooted stress. The result is a stronger, more vital physiology capable of resisting stress and maintaining better health. In the next chapter we will explore the implications of the Transcendental Meditation program on behavior by examining *dharma*, an important but misunderstood concept in Yoga philosophy.

6

Yoga and Dharma: Living Life in Accord with Nature's Design

In Chapter 1 we encountered Arjuna, standing in his chariot surveying the assembled armies and lamenting his impending decision. Should he participate in the upcoming battle, in accord with his duty as a warrior? If so, he would uphold the kingdom but would kill his relatives and teachers in the process, causing him untold grief. On the other hand, if he withdrew he'd be neglecting his duty to protect those he held dear. Certainly a challenging dilemma.

But subsequently we read of Lord Krishna's advice that the key to successful action is to transcend, experience Yoga, and then "perform action." His point was that to better deal with life's challenges we must dive deep within and access our infinite creativity and intelligence, and live life on that basis.

This formula presents an ideal foundation for engaging any aspect of life, however mundane it may appear to be. Our consciousness — our creativity, intelligence, and happiness — is the fundamental ground upon which we interact with the world, and by developing it we can more effectively take on the innumerable challenges that come our way.

There is, however, a fascinating new layer to this story, which brings us to our next area of consideration in Yoga philosophy. When Arjuna spoke of his duty as a warrior, he was referring to his *dharma*, and while *dharma* may certainly be translated as "duty," it includes a much more profound understanding than simply our moral (or legal) obligation — it addresses our ability to conform with the laws of nature that uphold individual and collective growth and evolution.

Dharma as natural law

One of the difficulties in understanding the nuances of dharma is that there is no equivalent concept in western culture. We certainly understand legal and ethical commitments, but dharma is much more profound. Fathoming its subtlety requires an appreciation of our inherent connection to natural law and our capacity to experience the home of all the laws of nature as our own consciousness.

Since the ability to easily experience this inner reality has been elusive for many centuries, modern scholars and translators often dismiss dharma's ancient understanding and regard it as a loose collection of moral codes and precepts passed down from generation to generation. Thus we generally find it translated as *duty, righteousness, religion*, or the like. And while these often seem contextually appropriate, they fall well short of conveying the deeper, more profound sense of the term, leaving many elegant and important passages in Yoga literature lifeless and virtually meaningless.[1]

Maharishi provides an understanding of dharma that is consistent with its Sanskrit etymology* while also satisfying the varied contexts in which it appears. In his commentary on the Bhagavad-Gita, Maharishi defines dharma as

> that invincible power of nature which upholds existence. It maintains evolution† and forms the very basis of cosmic life. It supports all that is helpful for evolution and discourages all that is opposed to it.[2]

Thus in Maharishi's view dharma is the fundamental force of nature that sustains growth and progress, leading life inexorably forward. It is the influence that "upholds the universe,"[3] guiding and administering it at every turn, promoting worldly prosperity and spiritual freedom.[4] In this understanding, dharma not only guides human life and evolution, but also every activity of the world around us: the motion of the planets, the interactions of subatomic particles, the laws governing the migration of birds, etc.

Maharishi often equates dharma with natural law — the totality of all the individual laws governing the universe. Using this terminology, the following passage provides an important clarification of Maharishi's teaching — the ultimate goal to which dharma irrevocably leads us is perfection, life

---

* *Dharma* comes from the Sanskrit root *dhri*, which means to *hold, preserve,* or *maintain*. In this context it refers to the power upholding progress and evolution.

† Maharishi is not referring to evolution in the Darwinian sense, but to the dynamics through which life naturally progresses, ultimately toward higher states of consciousness.

in higher states of consciousness. This is the goal of life, and dharma, or natural law, is the mechanism for taking us there.

> The purpose of natural law is to evolve life to perfection, to take life to its source, which is the absolute, non-changing field of all possibilities. Even though each law has its own specific level of performance and activity, the responsibility of that law, seen in the sequence of all the laws of nature, is found to be in the direction of evolution towards more and more.[5]

"Laws of nature" refers to the unchangeable principles of nature's functioning, including those discovered by the sciences as well as those yet to be uncovered. Maharishi's point here is intriguing, for he explains that each law has a two-fold purpose: It has its own role — such as the law of gravity or a law governing one or more physiological processes — but it also has a larger purpose in supporting growth toward higher states of consciousness.

Laws of nature not only include principles underlying the functioning of the physical environment, but also those governing human behavior and interactions, as our conduct moves us either toward growth and evolution or against the flow of life. Maharishi emphasizes this point in the following passage, in which he explains how different laws, or dharmas, express themselves as modes of activity that promote evolution:

> '*Dharmas*', the plural of *dharma*, signifies the different powers of nature upholding different avenues of the way of evolution. They take expression as specific modes of activity or different ways of righteousness, which keep the whole

stream of life in harmony — every aspect of life being properly balanced with every other aspect — and moving in the direction of evolution.[6]

Intuitively we know that some behavior is helpful to progress and some isn't. Conduct that includes courtesy, generosity, and aiding others in need, for example, is considered "good behavior," while rudeness, anger, aggression, and violence are generally considered "poor behavior." Why is one favorable and the other not? In Maharishi's account it is because one is conducive to growth and evolution while the other encourages stress and other impediments to progress.*

What does dharma mean in my life?
The difficulty, of course, is that the above examples are obvious, but often we can't foresee the outcomes of our choices. How are we to know whether we are acting in accord with dharma or against it? Even though we may hold the most sincere desire to behave properly, life can be complicated, and knowing the consequences of every action is beyond the scope of the intellect. This was true for the ancient heroes of the Vedic epics, such as Arjuna, as well as for us in the twenty-first century: They wanted, and we also want, happiness, success, prosperity, and freedom from poor decisions

---

* There is growing support within the scientific community for this understanding. While there is no consensus, many believe that happiness alone will create beneficial neurochemicals that support the physiology, whereas angry or hostile thoughts create damaging neurochemicals.

and unfortunate choices. But even when we try to carefully consider all angles we sometimes choose unsuitable friends, enter a profession that no longer fits our changing interests, attend a school that doesn't help us grow and progress, or we might even take bad advice. Or perhaps in our desire to be helpful we attempt to guide a friend, with disastrous consequences.

Societies try to help by upholding standards of behavior, either by way of formalized legislation, or through codes and conventions passed down within traditional cultures and religions. While these may be beneficial, most of our personal decisions go far beyond rules and traditions — they deal with choices, and choices within choices, and usually we have little knowledge of all potential outcomes. We may take a direction that is legal and acceptable to our religious faith and social customs, but which still creates problems and misfortune. For example, we might embark upon a career with great hopes and expectations, but which unexpectedly becomes unsuitable to our health and disposition, or which brings unhappiness and hardship. The choice may not have been illegal or immoral, but it was wrong if it inhibited our progress and wellbeing.

The Vedic tradition of knowledge, from which the science of Yoga comes, offers a criterion for correct behavior and decision-making that is conceptually simple and intellectually satisfying — right action fosters growth and evolution, while wrong action impedes progress. This understanding encompasses every type of decision regardless of the intricacy of its legal, moral, or ethical issues: Harming others hurts our own progress; damaging the environment creates unfavorable consequences for ourselves and for future generations; choosing relationships poorly may bring adverse influences into our lives; eating unhealthy food may impede our development of consciousness.

But the question remains: How can we make decisions that promote growth and evolution and avoid those that don't if we're not always able to foresee the consequences?

The answer lies in our relationship with the laws of nature themselves. Pure consciousness, we have seen, is the most fundamental level of nature's functioning. From this unbounded field of intelligence the laws of nature — the fundamental principles of nature's functioning, such as gravity and the laws governing our physiology — silently administer every part of creation. These laws of nature are known collectively as natural law.

And where can pure consciousness be found? It is our own inner Self, the source of our creativity and intelligence, the wellspring from which our thoughts and desires, our hopes, dreams, and aspirations emerge. It is deep within us, hidden like a vast underground ocean. When enlivened in our awareness, however, all of nature's administrative power becomes available to organize our life. In other words, the same intelligence that created and maintains the universe begins to calculate every possible implication of every possible act, laying out a course so that we can effortlessly and automatically move through life toward greater progress and prosperity. For one who is fully grounded in this field — who is *established in Yoga* — this cosmic computer becomes the guiding force, inspiring us to act in a way that is always positive, always life-supporting, and never damaging to ourselves, those around us, or the environment.

At first glance, it may seem as though striving to behave in accord with dharma entails giving our decisions over to some external power rather than living our own life and making our own decisions. In reality, however, the field of dharma is the most fundamental level of our own intelligence — it is our Self — and therefore living in accord with dharma simply means engaging our inherent potential to properly organize our life. In taking recourse to dharma, we *are* creating our own destiny, but from a much more powerful and profound level.

Personal dharma

The understanding of dharma as the laws of nature guiding progress and success has profound implications, not only for our ability to make appropriate, life-supporting decisions, but also for the fundamental way in which we conduct our lives. At every moment we are subject to laws of nature that influence our behavior, physiology, interaction with the environment, etc. Some may be the same for everyone — such as laws guiding general standards of behavior or those that direct physiological functioning — but there are also laws that pertain to a unique individual dharma, a natural path in life suitable for our own progress and not necessarily for others. This dharma may change at different times depending upon need, but there is always some unique course that helps us progress most easily toward more success and happiness, and ultimately to higher states of consciousness.

As a small child, of course, our dharma is to grow and learn, and as a youth it may be to attend school and learn even more. But in adulthood we must settle upon a profession or direction that will support our growth and evolution. This isn't a mysterious concept — many people feel naturally inclined toward a specific career path, such as painting, composing music, fixing automobiles, defending the nation, or upholding the law. For some the appropriate direction is more obvious than anything else in their life, but for others it may seem hidden behind a thick fog. The trick is to locate it.

"What is my dharma?", then, is an easy question to answer if you have a passion — if all you ever wanted was to cook gourmet meals or study weather patterns, or follow some dream. For those who don't feel such strong inclinations, the search may seem difficult, but in reality it is quite simple: Practice Yoga, dive deep within, unfold your own pure creative intelligence, and then the quiet whisper that may have been inaudible will begin to guide your life appropriately. This simple formula is available to everyone.

Violation of natural law

When we are in tune with dharma — with natural law — there is more progress and fulfillment, but when we violate a law or laws there are consequences: We create the ground for suffering. This may mean poor health (from eating unhealthy food), an unhappy friendship (from a bad decision), or a cold or flu (from not dressing properly in cold weather). Any of these may result in stress in the nervous system, which inhibits the development of consciousness. We might not notice the effect, but whatever slows the process of evolution creates a kind of suffering, because progress becomes slower and fulfillment is delayed.

Violation of a law of nature in this context doesn't mean breaking a law. From a scientific point of view a law of nature is inviolable — it is true in any circumstance and therefore cannot be broken. Violating natural law means acting inappropriately in the context of a law or laws. For example, if you stay out too long in the sun you may get burned. It doesn't matter that you had good intentions or that you didn't know the sun could be harmful — the reality is that you acted inappropriately with respect to the environmental conditions, and that resulted in suffering.

In Maharishi's view we unwittingly violate many laws of nature every day. These may include the obvious, such as unkind behavior or binging on junk food, but we also violate subtle laws that we aren't even aware of, and this impedes progress. Even having a profession that is not in accord with dharma hinders our growth. If it's my nature to be a gardener but I'm in sales, then I'm out of dharma, and progress may be slower and happiness less. It doesn't mean I'm a bad person, but it does suggest that I'm not capable of acting spontaneously in accord with every level of natural law.

We accept such shortcomings because we've never been presented with an alternative. It's always been our experience that certain parts of life are unknowable, certain events are random, and so we tend to hold the attitude that life is "just like that." But even though most of life is unknown and unforeseen, there is now a new possibility: If we take advantage of dharma — if we engage the intelligence that manages the universe — we can spontaneously live a more fulfilling and more progressive life, with fewer mistakes and unforeseen consequences. That is life in accord with dharma.

Is there scientific evidence?

Science seeks to understand reality, whatever that may be. It endeavors to comprehend how the universe works, and why individuals and societies behave as they do. Through its various disciplines, scientists have accumulated a vast body of understanding of the laws governing different aspects of life, using sophisticated methodologies appropriate to each discipline.

In many cases, scientists can study an object directly. If a new rock is discovered, a geologist may examine its chemical structure, its history, potentially gaining insights into the history of the earth, changes in climate over time, and geological trends. But often a scientist may study something that is not available to the senses — it may be unseen, untouchable, infinitesimally small, or it may be a force without substance. In such cases the scientist will formulate a hypothesis and then create studies that test whether the results are consistent with theory.

Galileo, for example, showed that gravitation accelerates all objects at the same rate, regardless of size. How did he measure an abstract force? Supposedly by dropping different-sized balls off the tower of Pisa, thus demonstrating that their speed of descent was the same. You can't see gravity, you can't touch it, but you can perform experiments that measure how it influences the universe.

Similarly, Maharishi's theory that you can learn to act spontaneously in accord with dharma does not lend itself to direct investigation, but you can design studies that will either support or not support the theory. For example, if we examine behavioral changes in those who practice Yoga, we can determine if these changes are more, or less, consistent with a working definition of "life in accord with dharma." There may be competing hypotheses, of course, but we'll at least see if the theory stands up to the empirical evidence.

Let's examine a few studies on individuals practicing the Transcendental Meditation program to see whether they exhibit a trend in the direction of more progressive, more positive, more intelligent, and more harmonious behavior — all characteristics Maharishi associated with life in accord with natural law.

In these studies the participants were never counseled on the nature of good or bad behavior. They were never told of the risks of substance abuse or the dangers of a criminal life, nor were they lectured on morality, ethics, or life in accord with natural law. They merely learned a simple meditation technique, nothing more, and their benefits arose spontaneously.

How, then, can we explain their more appropriate behavior? The simplest explanation is that they became more in tune with natural law, spontaneously and effortlessly. The mechanisms for this may well have been the release of stress, greater clarity of mind, increased intelligence and creativity, or more orderly brain functioning, all leading to better judgment. But the bottom line is that the research supports Maharishi's prediction that practicing the Transcendental Meditation technique and experiencing the state of Yoga enables us to function spontaneously more in accord with natural law. Let's look at a few examples.

Improved moral decisions

A principal goal of every educational system, whether stated or implied, is to develop moral maturity. We want our children to grow into adults who respect others, who care about the welfare of their community and the world, and who take responsibility for society and for those less fortunate. And we hope our children will understand what it means to be honest and straightforward and to aspire to appropriate moral and ethical decisions.

Scientific research indicates that fulfilling this lofty educational goal is well within reach. In one study, university students who took the Transcendental Meditation course showed significantly higher levels of moral maturity than control students. This study also measured students who were intending to take the course and found that their level of moral maturity was comparable to those not planning to learn, thus indicating that the higher scores among the Transcendental Meditation participants resulted from their practice.[7]

Other studies have produced similar findings. Researchers have documented how higher levels of EEG coherence found during Transcendental Meditation practice are associated with more principled moral reasoning (along with higher creativity, higher verbal intelligence, greater efficiency in learning new concepts, less neuroticism, and greater neurological efficiency).[8] In other words, as the brain becomes more orderly, behavior spontaneously improves — we make more appropriate decisions and behave more respectfully to others. Another study confirmed this finding when researchers found a significant correlation between EEG coherence from Transcendental Meditation practice and high levels of moral development.[9]

Reduced behavioral problems

Transcendental Meditation practice has also been used effectively to improve child behavior. In one study, adolescent children with high normal systolic blood pressure were randomly assigned to either take the Transcendental Meditation course or participate in a health education control group. After just four months, those practicing the Transcendental Meditation technique demonstrated decreased absenteeism, decreased school rule infractions, and decreased suspension days.[10]

In another study, school students with attention deficit hyperactivity disorder (ADHD) who learned the Transcendental Meditation technique showed improvement after three months on measures of executive function, indicating greater cognitive capability and self-control.[11]

The Transcendental Meditation program was also found effective as a method of improving the behavior of juvenile offenders. In one study, parents reported that their children's social behavior improved significantly as a result of their meditation.[12]

Results in prison rehabilitation programs

If we're looking for people with a history of poor decisions, a prison population is a good place to start, as prisoners have a demonstrated tendency to make seriously poor choices. Prisons offer a variety of rehabilitation programs, including vocational training, prison education, and counseling, but historically these programs have had little effect.[13] Nonetheless, prisoners have responded extraordinarily well to Transcendental Meditation practice in a number of settings. In one example, maximum security inmates displayed a marked decrease in negativism, verbal hostility, tendency to assault, resentment, and suspicion,[14] while in another study prisoners showed decreased aggression and increased self-development.[15]

A most significant finding is the apparent decrease in recidivism among prisoners who have taken the Transcendental Meditation course. Recidivism measures the rate of inmates' return to prison, which according to a recent study by the Pew Center on the States was 43.3% in 2004. Although this figure is only slightly higher than in 1999, it is misleading because during this period recidivism for new crime increased dramatically (over 11%) but was offset by a decrease in returns for technical parole violations.[16]

A study conducted through the California Department of Corrections found that parolees who took the Transcendental Meditation course during their incarceration showed significantly decreased recidivism over a five-year period after release. They also received fewer new prison terms after one year of their release and also between six months to six years after release.[17] In a separate study, maximum security inmates who took the Transcendental Meditation course showed a reduction of between 29% and 42% in their rate of return to prison after thirty-six months or more, in comparison to random samples of participants of four other prison rehabilitation programs.[18]

These prisoners were not counseled by their Transcendental Meditation teachers on how to behave. No one gave them lectures on natural law and how to act more in accord with dharma. They learned to meditate and their behavior improved spontaneously. It's a truly remarkable result of their practice.

Decreased cigarette, alcohol, and drug consumption
Substance abuse is a major problem in most modern societies, with well-known and well-publicized damage to both individual and community. The effects are severe, and include health problems, social difficulties, physical injury, violent and criminal behavior, vehicular accidents, and homicide. Substance abuse is thought to be influenced by genetic predisposition, environment, and internal psychological difficulties.

In one study, patients seeking treatment for traumatic stress who took the Transcendental Meditation course reduced their alcohol consumption significantly as compared to others undergoing psychotherapy.[19] In addition, a meta-analysis of all relevant studies found that individuals who had been using illegal drugs showed a substantial and long-lasting reduction after learning the Transcendental Meditation program. These reductions far exceeded the results of standard prevention programs for drug use.[20]

Studies have also found that cigarette and liquor consumption decrease spontaneously after a surprisingly short period of Transcendental Meditation practice.[21] In a study conducted by the Japanese National Institute of Industrial Health, researchers found an increase in the number of workers free from smoking among those who took the Transcendental Meditation course.[22]

In addition, a meta-analysis compared all research studies on the Transcendental Meditation program related to cigarette smoking with meta-analyses of standard treatment and prevention programs for smoking, and found a significantly greater reduction of cigarette use among those practicing the Transcendental Meditation program.[23] The same study compared a meta-analysis of all research studies on the Transcendental Meditation technique related to alcohol use with meta-analyses of standard alcohol treatment and prevention programs, finding a significantly greater reduction of alcohol use among those who practice the Transcendental Meditation technique.[24]

As we can see, the Transcendental Meditation program is a profoundly effective tool for both substance and criminal rehabilitation. It's worth reminding ourselves, however, that it is not exclusively for rehabilitation — it is a technique for experiencing Yoga and unfolding the total potential of life in higher states of consciousness. But because it profoundly affects every level of mind and body, it is a powerful program for solving many of life's fundamental challenges.

Studies on collective consciousness

In Chapter 9 we will examine research showing how entire societies can live more in accord with dharma. We'll see how efficiently large meditating groups can reduce crime, accidents, sickness rates, and even terrorism for whole populations. These groups used the Transcendental Meditation technique along with its advanced TM-Sidhi program.

7
The Fulfillment of Yoga in Higher States of Consciousness

The state of Yoga is the union of individual awareness with the inner Self, infinite pure consciousness. Through Transcendental Meditation practice, anyone can dive deep within and experience the creativity, intelligence, and bliss inherent within Yoga. But a question may arise: Since the state of Yoga is the object of meditation — in a sense, anyway — is the purpose of Yoga practice fulfilled when one experiences the inner Self?

Maharishi responds that there is much more to the story, for even with the experience of Being, "the overall purpose of Yoga [practice] is not yet satisfied."[1] So what still needs to be accomplished?

The short answer is that with regular Transcendental Meditation practice, the pure consciousness experienced during meditation begins to appear outside, permeating every aspect of our life. When the unbounded, eternal, blissful Self is never lost in any phase of life, *then* we find the fulfillment of Yoga practice. This is the experience of higher states of consciousness, the subject of this chapter.

Established in Yoga perform action

Shortly after exhorting Arjuna to experience Yoga, Lord Krishna described a new, enlightened state of consciousness as the most appropriate platform for life's activities:

योगस्थः कुरु कर्माणि सङ्गं त्यक्त्वा धनंजय
सिद्ध्यसिद्ध्योः समो भूत्वा समत्वं योग उच्यते

*Yogasthaḥ kuru karmāṇi sangam tyaktwā Dhananjaya
siddhyasiddhyoḥ samo bhūtwā samatwaṃ yoga uchyate*
(Bhagavad-Gītā, 2.48)

Established in Yoga, O Winner of Wealth, perform actions having abandoned attachment and having become balanced in success and failure, for balance of mind is called Yoga.

Understanding ancient texts can be tricky because we view them through the eyes of their translators and commentators, who often reflect a distorted or incorrect understanding. This verse in particular has been misunderstood in modern commentaries, but it is critical to our study of Yoga philosophy.

Established in Yoga does not refer to an attitude or idea of equanimity, as many suggest. Nor does it mean that one should take recourse to devotional practices or to a philosophy of selfless service. In Maharishi's view it describes one who has not only experienced the state of Yoga, but who permanently lives it — who, over time, has developed the capacity to spontaneously maintain pure consciousness as a constant feature of their waking consciousness.[2] This means that while one goes through the day attending to responsibilities, interacting with friends and family, and doing whatever one does, the unbounded, blissful Yoga is never lost. One may be an architect, lawyer, gardener, or anything — it doesn't matter, Yoga is always there. Not as an idea or a mood of Yoga, but the real thing.

Lord Krishna further commented that Arjuna should *perform actions having abandoned attachment and having become balanced in success and failure*. As Maharishi explains in his commentary, Lord Krishna was not suggesting that Arjuna adopt an attitude of non-attachment to success or failure. This is an unfortunate interpretation of modern commentators, which has led to monumental misunderstandings about Yoga. Creating a mood of non-attachment is not, as Maharishi points out, a sound basis for a practical life, and only serves to divide the mind and create a defeatist attitude.

Lord Krishna was instead describing a natural characteristic of the infinite fulfillment of higher states of consciousness. He was in essence saying that when the awareness is established in Yoga one will spontaneously experience boundless happiness, so profound and powerful that the gains and losses of life cannot shake it.[3] Indeed, one can be truly balanced in success and failure only when inner fulfillment is completely established, a state of life analogous to that of a billionaire who is not overshadowed by the losses and gains of a few hundred dollars.

Let's examine Maharishi's analysis of higher states of consciousness, so that we can better understand the details of this profound and important benefit of Yoga practice, and how it can impact our lives.

Seven states of consciousness

In his lectures and writings, Maharishi often spoke of seven states of consciousness — three "relative" states, so called because of their ever-changing character, and four "higher" states, each with its own unique characteristics. We are all familiar with the relative states: waking, deep sleep, and dreaming. These are scientifically defined in terms of their subjective experience along with specific physiological correlates.

The higher states, however, may be less familiar. Maharishi defines four, which he termed Transcendental Consciousness, Cosmic Consciousness, God Consciousness, and Unity Consciousness.

The fourth state: Transcendental Consciousness

When the mind goes deep within during Transcendental Meditation practice, it becomes increasingly still, increasingly peaceful. In its quietest state, it is completely silent yet fully awake, with no thought, mood, or intellectual activity. This is a state of pure knowingness, completely "self-referral" in the sense that the awareness is open only to itself — it is pure, infinite, unbounded wakefulness. In this state, the mind has transcended all limits of thought and is left by itself in the state of pure consciousness.[4] This is Transcendental Consciousness, which is essentially a more modern term for Yoga, the union of individual mind with Being. We have already covered the state of Yoga extensively in Chapters 1 and 3 for both experience and scientific evidence.

The fifth state: Cosmic Consciousness

With regular practice of the Transcendental Meditation technique, we not only experience the silence and peace within, but these same qualities begin to grow outside of meditation — we begin to feel more peaceful, silent, clear-minded, creative, etc. Even in extremely dynamic lifestyles that involve constant work and intense pressure, we naturally enjoy these qualities, especially as they deepen over time. These indicate that Yoga is beginning to grow in our lives.

One reason these qualities are experienced outside of meditation is that the deep rest we gain during Transcendental Meditation practice eliminates accumulated stress, resulting in a more normally functioning nervous system. As stress is dissolved, the nervous system becomes better able to experience pure consciousness along with dynamic activity. The short-term benefit is greater calm, clearer thinking, lower blood pressure, along with a host of other benefits well documented in the scientific literature. Over time, however, regular meditation gradually enhances the nervous system's flexibility so that it can simultaneously maintain Transcendental Consciousness along with the three relative states. In the following excerpt Maharishi explains:

> This is brought about by the mind gaining alternately transcendental consciousness and the waking state of consciousness, passing from one to the other. This gradual and systematic culture of the physical nervous system creates a physiological situation in which the two states of consciousness exist together simultaneously.[5]

When the nervous system is completely free of stress and able to fully support Transcendental Consciousness concurrently with waking, dreaming, and deep sleep, one enjoys a fifth state of consciousness. Maharishi calls this Cosmic Consciousness, because it includes the infinite value of Transcendental Consciousness along with the finite experience of our normal lives. Maharishi explains in his *Science of Being and Art of Living*:

> When this Self-consciousness is not lost, even when the mind comes out of the transcendent and engages itself once more in the field of activity, then the Self-consciousness gains the status of cosmic consciousness. The Self-consciousness is then eternally established in the nature of the mind. Even when the mind is awake, dreaming, or in deep sleep, the Self-consciousness is naturally maintained and is said to be cosmic consciousness.[6]

The characteristic of Cosmic Consciousness perhaps most challenging to understand is the coexistence of two levels of awareness, for how can one simultaneously maintain both silence and activity? How can a trader on the Chicago Commodities Exchange feel silent in the midst of a hectic day of buying and selling futures? How can a machinist working in a noisy shop feel silence? And how can a parent feel peaceful even while engaged in the busy activities of raising children?

We often maintain different levels of awareness at the same time, but it is so natural that we take it for granted. For example, when you go to work the day after your daughter delivers your first grandchild your daily activities will be suffused with joy. Even if work doesn't go well that day, it probably won't overshadow your happiness. In this situation two levels of awareness naturally coexist. Your work may dominate the mind but your profound happiness is always in the background. Similarly, athletes often report that during peak performances they feel a deep silence while running full speed up and down a court.

Both of these are examples of different levels of awareness functioning concurrently. In the same way, when living in Cosmic Consciousness there is an eternal, unshakable connection with the infinite bliss, silence, and peace within, which provides a powerful state of self-sufficiency and freedom to every facet of life.

A defining characteristic of Cosmic Consciousness is that the Self is experienced as separate from activity — infinite pure consciousness is a witness to everything. This is not a state of dissociation, but of greater integration — one functions more effectively and appropriately in the environment, while the Self remains infinitely free. In the following comment, Maharishi explains how the growth of Cosmic Consciousness results in a deeper appreciation of objects in the environment, even while the mind remains absorbed in pure consciousness:

> When, through the practice of Transcendental Meditation, cosmic consciousness has been gained, and the individual ego has expanded to cosmic status, the mind automatically functions from the level of its full potentiality and the senses, having reached their maximum development, function at their highest capacity. The objects of sense, however, remain in their unchanged state. That is why the senses, acting from their raised level, experience objects more completely, resulting in an even greater appreciation of the objects and thus providing experience of greater happiness on the sensory level. This creates a situation in which the objects of sense are enjoyed more thoroughly than before, but because Being is more fully grounded in the very nature of the mind, the impressions of sensory experience fail to capture the mind.[7]

Maharishi brings up a critical feature of this enlightened state when he writes of how the deepening of experience coincides with a decrease in attachment to objects in the material world. In practical terms, this means that one has an enhanced capacity to enjoy all aspects of life without the limitations of attachment. One may enjoy a beautiful sunset, for example, but there is no sorrow when the sun is gone and the experience has passed.

This quality of experience is fully enjoyed in Cosmic Consciousness, but its symptoms begin even in the early days of practice. Students often return to their Transcendental Meditation teachers after just a few meditation sessions exclaiming that already their day went more smoothly, coherently, and that they felt peaceful and unaffected by stressful situations. In one example, an attorney in a high-pressure practice, who had learned the Transcendental Meditation technique to combat excessive stress in her job, remarked to her teacher that after just a week or two she was no longer overwhelmed by the day's intense negotiations. She was amazed, however, that she wasn't apathetic. She was fully engaged, fully intent, but no longer tense or upset.

Such benefits are appealing to people in all walks of life. Often those with extremely dynamic professions — such as athletes, surgeons, or law enforcement officials — take the Transcendental Meditation course simply to enjoy the growth of silence, so that they can better deal with the stress inherent in their professions. Their interest may lie less in cultivating higher states of consciousness and more in the enhancement of enjoyment and success, but nonetheless the benefits that they receive, however practical, are fundamentally the symptoms of growing Cosmic Consciousness.

This brings us to an important element of our discussions on Yoga. We recall Maharishi's definition of Yoga as the union of the mind with pure consciousness. One level of Yoga is the experience of the inner Self during meditation, but the ability to spontaneously maintain pure consciousness permanently in higher states of consciousness represents what Maharishi referred to as the mature state of Yoga:

> Yoga, or Union of the mind with the divine intelligence, begins when the mind gains transcendental consciousness; Yoga achieves maturity when this transcendental bliss consciousness, or divine Being, has gained ground in the mind to such an extent that, in whatever state the mind finds itself, whether waking or sleeping, it remains established in the state of Being.[8]

Thus, one living in Cosmic Consciousness is also experiencing a state of Yoga.

Self-sufficiency is an important feature of Cosmic Consciousness that begins to grow even in the earliest days of practice. In Cosmic Consciousness, the experience of infinite peace, infinite bliss, and unbounded awareness is so fulfilling that nothing can shake it. Like the attorney mentioned above, one doesn't feel detached and uninterested, but rather one takes greater delight in all phases of life. At the same time, however, unexpected losses or disappointments cannot overshadow the peace and joy and the knowledge that the goal of life has been achieved.

In the last chapter, we discussed action in accord with dharma, natural law, and now we can tie this understanding to our consideration of higher states of consciousness. When we learn the Transcendental Meditation technique, we begin to establish our awareness in the home of all the laws of nature, the field of dharma. As consciousness grows, we increasingly act in accord with dharma, and when we reach Cosmic Consciousness every act, every decision, is always in tune with natural law, never damaging to ourself or to others.

The sixth state: God Consciousness

Cosmic Consciousness is a state of perfect harmony and self-sufficiency, and is so fulfilling that it might seem like the ultimate attainment of human life — as though the development of human consciousness had reached its peak. But this is not the case, for Maharishi describes additional states that represent even higher levels of development.

As mentioned earlier, a feature of Cosmic Consciousness is the experience of complete fulfillment: The heart — the aspect of the mind responsible for feelings and emotions — is eternally and unshakably content. Even though fulfilled within itself, however, it begins to move, it begins to flow in waves of love toward everything. It is as though the silent ocean of love rises up in waves, not as a mood or an idea but as the spontaneous and natural expression of the infinite bliss within. In his *Science of Being and Art of Living*, Maharishi gives us a profound and beautiful description of the flow of love that begins in Cosmic Consciousness:

> Here is the unbounded flow of love — at the sight of everything, at the hearing of everything, at the smelling of anything, at the tasting of anything, at the touch of anything. But entire life in its multifarious diversity is nothing but fullness of love, bliss, and contentment — eternal and absolute.[9]

This flow of love cultures both body and mind, and in particular the senses through which we experience the world. As the outward expression of love grows, perception through the five senses becomes increasingly refined and one begins to appreciate subtler values of the material world. Over time, as perception becomes ever more subtle, one begins to perceive the finest level of creation, which Maharishi describes as celestial because it is suffused with a kind of golden light.[10]

Maharishi calls this state God Consciousness because one is capable of appreciating the entire range of material creation, from its surface to its most subtle level. As in Cosmic Consciousness, one experiences the unbounded, infinite, cosmic Self, but in God Consciousness the outer experience includes perception on its most refined level. And just as one best understands an artist by appreciating his or her art, in God Consciousness one fully appreciates every level of creation, and is therefore better able to appreciate its creator.

Maharishi often compared the experience of God Consciousness to the view of a stand of trees at sunset. Our perception of the trees is to some extent determined by where we are standing: If the trees are between us and the sun, they will appear normal, which is analogous to the visual experience of Cosmic Consciousness. But if we are standing between the trees and the setting sun, they will appear lit up with a golden light, which is analogous to the experience of celestial perception in God Consciousness.

In God Consciousness one feels infinite joy in every experience. One experiences the harmony of every object of perception, and even though one still perceives the differences — between the lawn and the house, between each human being — one also enjoys a growing sense of unity, which culminates in the seventh state of consciousness.

The seventh state: Unity Consciousness

It is the nature of love to unite, and the infinite love rising in the heart in God Consciousness becomes the means for unfolding a seventh state of consciousness, which Maharishi termed Unity Consciousness. In Cosmic Consciousness the awareness is infinite, unbounded, and though one is completely fulfilled there is nonetheless a kind of duality — it is as though "I am separate from the world around me. I am a witness to my every thought and action, and to all activity." In this state the mind lives in a state of eternal freedom, and

> remains unbounded by what it experiences during all the activity of the outside relative world. This state of freedom from the bondage of experience gives the mind the status of cosmic consciousness, the state of eternal freedom in any of the relative states of life — waking, dreaming, or sleeping.[11]

In this state, the Self is no longer overshadowed by, or identified with, objects of experience — it is self-sufficient, a silent witness. In God Consciousness, however, this gap begins to close. When the heart in its state of eternal contentment begins to move, it draws everything together, simply because that is the nature of love; and this drawing together closes the "gap" between the Self and the material world. This is the mechanism for unfolding Unity Consciousness, in which the appreciation of the finest celestial level expands to include its transcendental value.

As we have seen throughout these chapters, the underlying basis of every object is the same pure consciousness that we find within us. In Unity Consciousness we spontaneously connect the two: We experience that the infinite intelligence underlying all creation is the same eternal, unbounded consciousness that is the Self — that the environment we see, touch, smell, taste, and hear is an expression of our own Self. Unity Consciousness is the highest level of human achievement, for in this state the natural experience is that everything we perceive is an expression of our inner nature.[12]

In the beginning days of Unity Consciousness, we experience the immediate object of perception as an expression of our Self. Our usual experience, however, is that there are layers of perception. There is an object directly in front, maybe others off to the side, and more in the background. As Unity Consciousness matures, the secondary levels of perception also begin to be appreciated in terms of our Self, and eventually the entire field of perception and all that exists is included.[13] Maharishi describes this as a state of total knowledge — "knowledge" because it is the direct cognition, the direct experience, of the ultimate reality of life; the entire field of relative life is nothing other than pure consciousness, our own Self.

This experience is known in Sanskrit as *Brahm*, Totality. Maharishi describes Brahm as the experience of everything in terms of wholeness — one great, grand totality of everything that is and was, on the practical level of daily living.

When someone experiencing Brahm perceives the environment, there are still birds and trees, planets and stars, but the differences between them are less, while unity predominates. Brahm is a concrete experience, not an intellectual idea, philosophic orientation, or opinion — it is the profound appreciation of the reality of the unity of life.

This state is the most fully mature state of Yoga, the fulfillment of Lord Krishna's encouragement to Arjuna that he perform action *established in Yoga*. While each of the higher states fulfills this ideal, it is in Brahm that one truly lives Unity, in which everything — to the far extent of the universe — is appreciated as an expression of one's own Self.[14] This is Yoga, this is fulfillment, the goal of human life, and as Maharishi so often exclaimed, it is "a life worth living."

Experiences of Unity Consciousness
The following are a few experiences from long-term practitioners of the Transcendental Meditation and TM-Sidhi program. In these we see a growing awareness that the world around is nothing other than an expression of Being, our inner Self. This is not an intellectual understanding, though that certainly follows, but a concrete experience that one's own Self is the ultimate reality of everyone and everything.

In this first experience, we see clear signs of growing God Consciousness, but also the simultaneous unfoldment of Unity. Maharishi has pointed out that higher states of consciousness can to some extent develop concurrently — while

Cosmic Consciousness is developing, one can also experience symptoms of God Consciousness and Unity Consciousness. The following five paragraphs represent one continuous experience.

> Increasingly my experience is that everything and everyone I encounter are experienced as nothing other than my own Self. This is especially clear when walking in the woods, but also apparent in town or anywhere. It seems that Being is shining and glistening and even smiling at me from the surface of everything.
>
> This is difficult to describe. How does one perceive Being in activity? It's as if the inner Being, the Self of everything, somehow rises to the surface and makes itself apparent.
>
> With this experience of becoming aware of my own Self in all things, love begins to flow — love without boundaries, without exceptions, without considerations of any sort. Love flows out towards all that I perceive and seems to flow back to me as well.
>
> This experience is simply an augmentation of the experience of Being that became a constant feature of my own waking, dreaming and sleeping awareness for the past two and a half years — just that the experience of Being has become ever more insistent, ever more dense around me and in my awareness, ever more powerful.
>
> Now, in addition to the daily, hourly experience of it in my own awareness, it has become apparent in all things.[15]

This experience provides us with several characteristics of growing higher states. In addition to the emerging quality of Unity, we see an example of refined perception and also the flow of love toward the environment. The experiencer also notes that he had been experiencing Being for two and a half years prior, seemingly a reference to the development of Cosmic Consciousness.

The next also illustrates growth toward Unity Consciousness. Here the experiencer indicates that everything in the environment is "an arrangement of my inner bliss."

> Opening my eyes after program [Transcendental Meditation and TM-Sidhi practice*], everything that I see I recognize as an arrangement of my inner bliss, my Self. It's just that simple — there is a warmth of recognition. Everything is exhibiting orderliness, sequence, symmetry, wholeness, which are all signs of my infinite Self. Everything is a little bit of me. Everything as such is dear, and yet not too important next to my unbounded Self.
>
> When seeing other people there is the quiet knowledge that "This is me," which accompanies the more intellectual recognition of the particular person. When speaking to others, there is a quiet feeling that I am the listener who is being spoken to by me — but that listener is not my ego or my intellect, it is the unbounded bliss. It is all very simple and natural, much simpler than these words.

The next experience again suggests growing Unity Consciousness, this time in terms of the basic structure of experience:

> During the Transcendental Meditation and TM-Sidhi programs, I experienced a sudden shift in perception, a fundamental change in the structure of experience: a unity of experiencer and object of experience in one integrated state of awareness. It is certainly the most captivating experience that I have ever had. Inner fullness now dominates my life.[16]

---

* We will discuss the TM-Sidhi program in detail in Chapter 8.

Experiences of Unity in the Upanishads

In Chapter 3 we read several selections from the Upanishads, which are the experiences of higher states of consciousness recorded by ancient *Rishis* (Seers). Following are a few expressions from the Upanishads that are especially appropriate in this context, as they provide a beautiful and compelling description of Brahm. In Sanskrit these are called *Mahavakyas* — *great expressions* — because they describe this exalted state of Unity. Although there are a number of *Mahavakyas* throughout the Upanishads, four of the principal ones are included here for the sake of illustration.

In the first selection, the Rishi expresses his identity with Brahm. He experiences Brahm in the sense that he is Brahm, he is the reality of all that there is and will ever be.

> अहं ब्रह्मास्मि
> *Ahaṃ Brahmāsmi*
>   (Bṛihad-Āraṇyak Upanishad, 1.4.10)
> *I am Totality.*[17]

Maharishi explains the purport of the next Mahavakya as "the obvious phase of phenomenal existence, which you take as yourself, is not your real nature — you, in fact, are That transcendental reality."[18]

> तत्त्वमसि
> *Tat Twam Asi*
>   (Chhāndogya Upanishad, 6.11)
> *Thou art that.*

Maharishi interprets the next as a description of the fully awake totality of individual consciousness, Brahm, which comprehends the infinite dynamism of the universe within the infinite silence of Self.[19]

प्रज्ञानं ब्रह्म

Pragyānaṃ Brahm
  (Aitareya Upanishad, 3.1.3)
Consciousness is Brahm.

In the following, the Rishi describes his experience that the inner Self (Atma) is appreciated as Brahm. This represents a deeper level of experience in which the totality of life is experienced as oneself.

अयम् आत्मा ब्रह्म

Ayam Ātmā Brahm
  (Māndukya Upanishad, 2)
This Self is Brahm.

These four expressions from the Upanishads provide a beautiful picture of the complete unfoldment of Unity Consciousness, which once attained can never be lost — it is the ultimate reality of life, the ultimate goal of human existence.

> No diversity of life is able to detract from this state of supreme Unity. One who has reached It is the supporter of all and everything, for he is life eternal. He bridges the gulf between the relative and the Absolute. The eternal Absolute is in him at the level of the perishable phenomenal world.[20]

The Bhagavad-Gita expresses this reality in the following verse:

आत्मौपम्येन सर्वत्र समं पश्यति योऽर्जुन
सुखं वा यदि वा दुःखं स योगी परमो मतः

*Ātmaupamyena sarvatra samaṃ pashyati yo Arjuna
sukhaṃ vā yadi vā duḥkhaṃ sa yogī paramo mataḥ*

(Bhagavad-Gita, 6.32)

He who sees everything with an even vision by comparison with the Self, be it pleasure or pain, he is deemed the highest yogi, O Arjuna.

By comparison with the Self, Maharishi explains in his commentary, means *in terms of his own Self.* This is the compact expression of Unity, which Maharishi goes on to describe as the highest level of human perfection:

> Yoga in this state has reached its perfection; there is no level of Union higher than this that he has gained. He stands established on the ultimate level of consciousness.[21]

In our next chapter we will examine the TM-Sidhi program, an advanced aspect of Transcendental Meditation practice that allows us to function on the level of Yoga, pure consciousness, thus enhancing growth toward higher states of consciousness.

8
The Transcendental Meditation-Sidhi Program

During Transcendental Meditation practice we learn to dive deep within and experience the state of Yoga, Transcendental Consciousness, the infinite, unbounded reservoir of energy, intelligence, and bliss at the source of thought. When we come out of meditation we feel fresher, rested, more alert, and more peaceful within, leading to the myriad benefits discussed in previous chapters. The Transcendental Meditation technique is extremely effective for the growth and evolution of consciousness, but in 1976 Maharishi introduced an advanced program that is even more powerful — the Transcendental Meditation-Sidhi program (TM-Sidhi program).

The effectiveness of the TM-Sidhi program stems from its ability to more rapidly integrate the deepest and most profound values of consciousness with the "surface" levels of the mind, a characteristic of the growth of higher states of consciousness.[1] During instruction, one learns to introduce various TM-Sidhi techniques and then bring the awareness back to the Self — to the unbounded awareness within.[2] From this simple practice, the effects of the techniques become a spontaneous reality, their success determined by the relative purity of the nervous system. Maharishi explained during a 1980 conference in Switzerland:

> While Transcendental Meditation opens the mind to the experience of Transcendental Consciousness, unbounded awareness, the TM-Sidhi techniques activate this silent level. Specific mental formulae are introduced as gentle impulses of thought during the experience of unbounded awareness. The mind then lets go of this gentle impulse and returns to the state of unbounded awareness. The result is experienced as the specific effect of the particular TM-Sidhi technique.[3]

Maharishi describes the mechanics in terms of enlivening different laws of nature. As we saw in Chapter 1, every natural law is contained within pure consciousness. A TM-Sidhi technique simply exercises the mind to act in accord with a particular law.[4] But while we might practice one of the Sidhi techniques to enliven a specific quality of mind or body — such as the enhancement of human emotions, or more sharp or refined hearing[5] — its ultimate goal is to accelerate the growth of higher states of consciousness by enabling us to function more and more from the level of Yoga, Transcendental Consciousness.

Yogic Flying

The most important TM-Sidhi technique promotes what Maharishi referred to as Yogic Flying, which according to the Patanjali Yoga Sutra, one of the principal texts of Yoga, results in the ability to move through the air at will. During Yogic Flying, practitioners enjoy powerful upsurges of bliss and energy, accompanied by high levels of brainwave coherence.

According to accounts in the Vedic literature, there are three stages of Yogic Flying.[6] During the first, the body lifts up and moves forward in short hops. In the second stage, the body hovers for short periods. In the third, one can move through the air by mental intention. Regardless of the outer experience, however, there is a profound enlivenment of pure consciousness in each stage, leading to a greater ability to behave spontaneously in accord with the laws of nature, as Maharishi explains:

> Regular practice of Yogic Flying leads the individual mind to enjoy control of Nature's central switchboard from where Natural Law governs the life of everyone and administers the entire universe from within the intelligence of every grain of creation.[7]

Maharishi here refers to pure consciousness as the "switchboard" from which each individual law of nature administers its area of responsibility. We "enjoy control" because when we identify the active awareness with its own inner nature, the mind gains the ability to perform in the same style that nature performs. In an excerpt from a different lecture, Maharishi elaborates this point:

> The functioning of transcendental pure consciousness is the functioning of natural law in its most settled state. The conscious human mind, identifying itself with this level of nature's functioning, gains the ability to perform in the style with which nature performs its activity at its most fundamental level. Completely identified in transcendental

consciousness with the full potential of natural law, the human mind is a field of all possibilities.[8]

The descriptions of *siddhi** practice found in the Patanjali Yoga Sutra have been poorly understood for centuries, and thought to involve arduous concentration and mental control. As a result, there has been little documentation of successful performance. In developing the TM-Sidhi program, however, Maharishi demonstrated that it is easy and automatic, and produces significant, scientifically measurable results. And the experiences of practitioners have been remarkable. Let's consider a sample of experiences, and then examine some of the research.

Experiences from the TM-Sidhi program

The following, from advanced TM-Sidhi practitioners, illustrate a profound level of experience cultured over years of practice.[9] It is important to remember, though, that even beginners generally have deep experiences in the first days of their practice. These become more powerful and blissful over time, as one continues to fathom the depths of Yoga.

> During the TM-Sidhi program my awareness was in pure consciousness. I kept experiencing indescribable bliss, an indescribable, ecstatic feeling that I felt could not be contained within myself. During Yogic Flying I felt the most blissful feeling I've ever felt in my life.

---

* The conventional transliteration of the Sanskrit is *siddhi* (with two "d"s) but Maharishi preferred a slightly modified spelling for his TM-Sidhi program (one "d") in order to distinguish it from previous modern attempts at *siddhi* performance.

In the next, the practitioner also describes a deep state of bliss:

> The overall experience is one of waves of blissful energy floating in their own eternal ocean. A wonderful realization that is growing in my awareness, especially during these Yogic Flying sessions, is that we are only bliss — perfectly coherent, infinitely silent, and dynamic all at the same time. Through repeated exposure to pure consciousness I realize that we have always been that eternally awake pure consciousness in its infinite dance of silence and dynamism.

Here a TM-Sidhi practitioner notes that the experiences are most pronounced during Yogic Flying:

> I experience deep silence, bliss, and unbounded love during my practice, and especially during Yogic Flying. In several [sessions], during Yogic Flying I felt that I am Brahm, which creates this world and enjoys and loves everything and everyone. During these experiences I felt very great power while flying.

In Chapter 7, when considering higher states of consciousness, we encountered the term Brahm as the supreme awakening of Unity Consciousness, the grand totality of wholeness. This experience is a beautiful example of growing Unity Consciousness.

The experience continues with an elaboration upon the quality of love. We may also recall from Chapter 7 that a characteristic of higher states of consciousness is the flow of infinite love.

> I felt unbounded love towards everyone and everything. In this moment I realized and felt the connection among

everything in the universe. I was a small part of the whole. Then an enormous wave of happiness and bliss poured onto me, because all of this was coming out of me and coming back in me, and all of this was me.

Another individual comments on the effulgent quality of pure consciousness. We may recall that a verse from the Upanishads also described the Self as effulgent (p. 29).

> The field of consciousness is also characterized by brightness, self-effulgence. It is an intense state of unity of experiencer and process of experience. There is a very subtle emanation of attention from the field of the self-referral Atma [the Self], which turns back on itself almost immediately without disconnecting from the totality or oneness of the field. This looping of attention produces a sense of the Totality flowing within Itself.

After an experience of unbounded awareness outside of meditation, a TM-Sidhi practitioner commented that

> This experience of unboundedness is beyond language — not possible to localize in the very tiny boundaries of speech, inexpressible.

Another long-term TM-Sidhi practitioner cited an experience of bliss in activity, which arose just after completing Yogic Flying. Experiences outside TM-Sidhi practice are especially important because they indicate an integration between the inner reality and outer life, a sign of the growth of higher states of consciousness.

> At the end of TM-Sidhi practice, after Yogic Flying, there are no thoughts in my mind, just bliss. This bliss has a dynamic aspect to it — like an infinite number of soft points of light flowing gently into a center, like water pouring into

a central point in my chest (like a cone). It is a huge, infinite phenomenon.

Practical application of the TM-Sidhi program

These experiences are deeply profound and certainly something to look forward to, but you might also wonder how such a practice can affect the more mundane elements of life. After all, you may have a job, responsibilities, and you may be interested in the practical, day-to-day outcome of this practice.

As it turns out, Maharishi's advanced program has attracted the attention of many research scientists who have investigated its immediate impact on both mind and body. One researcher, for example, found that subjects practicing Yogic Flying exhibited extraordinarily high levels of EEG coherence.[10] This has significant behavioral implications because EEG coherence has been correlated with growth of intelligence, improved creativity, higher academic achievement, and more principled moral reasoning.[11]

In a separate study, EEG alpha power (associated with restful alertness) during TM-Sidhi practice was significantly higher than during control conditions in which the same subjects imitated the movement of Yogic Flying. Alpha power was measured in all brain areas.[12] This is important because restful alertness is the spontaneous ability to maintain the silence of Transcendental Consciousness during activity. The growth of this quality enables one to be more calm and steady, and better able to deal with the dynamic flow of modern life.

Researchers have also determined that the number of months practicing the TM-Sidhi program is correlated with both higher intelligence and higher creativity.[13] In other words, the longer one practices the more these qualities grow.

Here are a few additional studies that indicate the development of potential from TM-Sidhi practice:

- A researcher, using an index of efficiency of concept learning, found that students who had taken the Transcendental Meditation course improved significantly in comparison to matched control students from the same university.[14] This study suggests that practitioners are better able to process information as a result of increased efficiency of their brain functioning.

- University students who learned the TM-Sidhi program demonstrated improvements in creativity, autonomy, and intrinsic spirituality, as well as growth in an overall measure of wellbeing and a measure of psychological integration.[15]

- Secondary students who took the TM-Sidhi course also increased in creativity over a nine-month period.[16]

In the next chapter, we'll examine a monumentally important application of the TM-Sidhi program — how it can help create world peace.

9
Creating World Peace Through Yoga

The inner Self is an unbounded ocean of peace, eternally silent, infinitely blissful. When we experience the Self during Transcendental Meditation practice, we feel inner peace, and as we continue to practice regularly we become naturally more peaceful — we begin to enjoy the unshakable ocean of silence and bliss even while engaged in the most dynamic activity. To live this state perpetually is the goal of human life: freedom, self-sufficiency, with no suffering of any kind.

We can see that individuals can live more peacefully within themselves — in fact this is a practical, scientifically verifiable reality. But can we create a violence-free, war-free world?

Maharishi's answer is yes, but he emphasizes that peace can never become a reality unless the individuals within a society are themselves peaceful, just as a forest can never be green unless its trees are green. This, of course, suggests that we will never be without war and violence until everyone is experiencing the state of Yoga and living peace within. But does that put world harmony out of reach? The prospect of teaching the Transcendental Meditation technique to every individual in every country is daunting, though certainly possible.

Fortunately, that's not the end of the story. From the earliest days of his teaching, Maharishi indicated that it is not necessary for everyone to practice his meditation. In a lecture in 1962, he predicted that a relatively few people practicing the Transcendental Meditation program would be sufficient to create an influence of harmony such that peace would become an automatic reality:

> My calculation is that the day one-tenth of the adult population of the world* begins to meditate a half-hour morning and evening and begins to emit an influence of peace and harmony from the deepest level of consciousness — from that day, the atmosphere of the world, this negative atmosphere of the world, will be neutralized, and from that day will dawn the chance of no war for centuries to come.[1]

Maharishi noted that we all impact the environment anyway. When one is filled with tension, stress, or even anger and hatred, those qualities permeate the surroundings, just as a harmonious, compassionate person will create a corresponding effect. The state of Yoga, however, presents a special case, for it is infinitely peaceful, harmonious, and coherent. In that state "the heart rests in eternal contentment and the mind is filled with the unity of life, where there is no trace of duality."[2] Thus as Yoga becomes increasingly part of our experience — both during Transcendental Meditation practice as well as afterward in activity — we create a progressively

---

✶ Maharishi later added that 10% of the population included a safety factor, but that 1% would be sufficient. One percent has since become the standard for research on the effects of the Transcendental Meditation program on society.

stronger influence of fulfillment, peace, and unity. And because that level of life is so much more powerful than the conscious level of the mind, even a few individuals — just 1% of a population — practicing Maharishi's meditation is enough to create an empirically verifiable effect in society.[3]

The Yoga Sutra also predicts a more harmonious, unifying influence in the environment from the experience of Yoga, stating that:

तत्सन्निधौ वैरत्यागः
Tat-sannidhau vaira-tyāgaḥ*
(Yoga Sutra, 2.35)
In the vicinity of Yoga, harmony prevails.[4]

This *sutra*† speaks to every level of Yoga. It is the reality of Transcendental Consciousness, of the growing integration of Yoga and activity, and of the mature states of Yoga in higher states of consciousness. In each case, there is a powerful influence on the environment, the impact of which depends upon the purity of the experience.

---

* The full text of the sutra is: *Ahimsā-pratishtāyām tat-sannidhau vaira-tyāgah*, which means *harmony prevails in the vicinity of one who is established in ahimsā (non-violence)*. We will discuss ahimsā in Chapter 11, where we will see that the translation of the entire sutra means essentially the same as this abbreviated version.

† *Sutra* refers either to a single, compact expression of knowledge, or else a compilation of many such expressions. Hence the Yoga Sutra is a collection of individual sutras on the subject of Yoga. Traditionally each individual sutra is the subject of extensive commentary that attempts to "unpack" the knowledge contained within it.

Maharishi first spoke of this effect in 1962, but it wasn't until 1974 that there were enough practitioners in US cities to test his hypothesis. Since that time, a number of studies have shown that when only 1% of the population of a city or town practices the Transcendental Meditation technique, positive trends begin to grow. In one study, researchers compared 24 "1% cities" with 24 matched control cities. When the number of practitioners reached the 1% threshold, crime rate decreased significantly over the next six years.[5] Through their statistical analysis, the researchers found that the effect cannot be explained by the major demographic variables generally associated with crime. This study thus shows that the practitioners created a positive effect on the environment that continued over time. In recognition of Maharishi's prediction, this 1% phenomenon has come to be known as the *Maharishi Effect*.

How can we account for this relationship between Transcendental Meditation practice and improvements in the quality of life? What are the mechanics through which these influences occur?

We can look at the effectiveness of the program in terms of its proximate effect, but Maharishi also introduced a theoretical explanation for the influence of the Maharishi Effect over large geographical areas — how, for example, a group of practitioners of sufficient size can influence the entire US. At the core of this understanding is the principle of collective consciousness.

Collective consciousness

We all have an intuitive understanding of individual consciousness. We know that each of us is awake, alert to varying degrees, and can experience the environment through the senses. Collective consciousness is simply the wholeness of consciousness, the sum of the consciousness of the members of any specific group. In Maharishi's words, "when we talk of community consciousness, we merely put together the consciousness of all the individuals who make up the community, or the nation."[6] There are innumerable levels of collective consciousness, but for practical purposes we can think of family, community, city, provincial, national, and world consciousness, each of which is created by its component individuals.

Maharishi describes a reciprocal relationship between individual consciousness and collective consciousness, such that "as individual consciousness grows, collective consciousness rises; and as collective consciousness rises, individual consciousness grows."[7] In other words, as we regularly experience pure consciousness and enliven it in our awareness, the levels of collective consciousness in which we participate — family, city, state — are simultaneously improved. This higher level of collective consciousness in turn affects each individual within that group.

For example: When people learn the Transcendental Meditation technique and practice it twice a day, they not only grow toward Cosmic Consciousness but also improve the collective consciousness of their family (along with their cities, states, etc.). This higher level of collective consciousness affects everyone else in the family, regardless of whether or not they practice the Transcendental Meditation technique. The effect may be relatively small if there is only one person in the family meditating, but if there are several then the effect becomes far more significant. And if 1% of their cities practice, then crime, accidents, and other negative features of life begin to disappear.

The role of TM-Sidhi practice in creating world peace
While the Transcendental Meditation technique is an impressive tool for improving the quality of life of both individual and society, the TM-Sidhi program is even more effective, because it teaches us to function from the level of Yoga. Its effect is therefore much stronger, so much so that Maharishi predicted that even smaller numbers — just the square root of 1% of a population — is sufficient to create a very powerful influence of peace and coherence.*

Another text from the Yoga tradition, known as the Shiva Samhita, records a similar prediction, stating that Yogic Flying will "destroy the darkness of the world":

---

* The square root of 1% was determined on the basis of the observation that other coherent systems in nature (such as laser beams and superconductors) rely on the increased orderliness of a similarly small proportion of their constituent elements to create coherence for the entire system.

योगी पद्मासनस्थोऽपि भुवमुत्सृज्य वर्तते
वायुसिद्धिस्तदा ज्ञेया संसारध्वान्तनाशिनी

Yogī padmāsanastho 'pi bhuvam utsṛijya vartate
vāyu-siddhis tadā gyeyā saṃsāra-dhvānta-nāshinī
(Shiva Saṃhitā, 3.42)

When the Yogi, rising into the air sitting in the lotus position, departs, then the Vayu-siddhi (Yogic Flying) is known as the destroyer of the darkness of the world.[8]

Darkness of the world can be interpreted variously, but eliminating negative trends in society such as crime, war, and terrorism certainly fulfills the prediction. Significantly, this verse singles out Yogic Flying among the various TM-Sidhi techniques, and indeed physiological research shows an unusually higher degree of brainwave coherence during its practice.

Since Maharishi first introduced the TM-Sidhi program in 1976, over 50 research projects — 23 of which have been published in peer-reviewed academic journals — have confirmed its effectiveness on every level of society. The following examples should give an idea of the range and scope of the studies:

Improved quality of life, Washington, DC: In June 1993, a project was organized to demonstrate the effect of the collective practice of the TM-Sidhi program. The organizers chose Washington, DC, both for its leadership role in national and international politics as well as its consistently high rate of violent crime. To document the results, the project leaders assembled an independent review board composed of leading social scientists and criminologists, to ensure that the effects of the project were scientifically documented in accordance with the highest standards of the social sciences.

Over the eight-week duration of the project, experts in TM-Sidhi practice gathered from all over the world, numbering almost 4,000 by the conclusion. Significantly, as the size of the group increased, violent crime diminished, reaching a 23% reduction by week eight.[9] Quality of life in Washington also improved, as measured by an index including reduced emergency psychiatric calls, reduced trauma, fewer complaints against police, and fewer accidental deaths.[10]

Researchers also measured bipartisanship between the two main political parties of the US government. Prior to the project the parties had been highly polarized, but once the conference was underway there was a significant increase in bipartisan voting patterns in both the Senate and House. This contrasted with the extreme divisiveness that marked voting patterns immediately prior to and immediately following the project. The researchers analyzed data of all roll-call votes in the House and Senate for 1994 as a control.[11]

Why was there an increase in bipartisanship during this period and not immediately before or after? The simplest explanation is that group practice of the TM-Sidhi program increased harmony and flexibility in the collective consciousness. The government, which Maharishi holds to be an innocent mirror of collective consciousness, merely reflected these qualities in its activities.[12]

Reduced regional conflict and greater progress towards peace: In October 1978, Maharishi sent experts in the TM-Sidhi program to the main regional trouble spots in Southeast Asia, the Middle East, southern Africa, and Central America to create a calming influence through their practice. During this time, in comparison to a baseline period prior to the project, analysis of data from an independent data bank showed reduced hostile acts and increased cooperative events in those areas and among the nations involved in the conflicts.[13]

The following is a brief description from a member of the group that went to Managua, Nicaragua, in the midst of a violent conflict between the government and rebel forces:

> When we first arrived, there was a palpable feeling of tension in the air. No one was smiling, no children were playing, and the local Nicaraguan citizens were bracing for more violence. The residents were extremely nervous, and unwilling to discuss the situation. Even though there was an attack planned for the next day upon the government compound (next door to our hotel), Maharishi told us to not worry — that in just one or two days everything would be quiet.
>
> Within two days the atmosphere completely changed. The rebel army held off its attack, and a few days later began negotiations with the government. Soon the press came piling into Managua (it had been too dangerous before), and the mood of the city became increasingly light-hearted, improving day-by-day. Children began playing in the streets, and there was a warm and friendly feeling in the air.

To be quite honest, I was stunned. I had been practicing the TM-Sidhi program for over a year, and though I'd had good experiences, the effect here was dramatic and unprecedented. All the hotel staff, from the manager to the housekeepers, were thrilled and completely understood what we had accomplished. The press, who had come to monitor the negotiations, interviewed us several times, wanting to know more about the effects of the Transcendental Meditation and TM-Sidhi program. The negotiations continued, but sadly we had to leave after a few months. Shortly after our departure the negotiations broke down and the violence resumed.

When we returned to the US we compared notes with friends who had gone to trouble spots in other parts of the world. They all had similar experiences — when they arrived the violence stopped, and when they departed it resumed after a short time.

Improved quality of life in Rhode Island: During the summer of 1978, a group of several hundred TM-Sidhi practitioners assembled in Rhode Island, US. During the project's time period, the quality of life in Rhode Island improved significantly compared to a control state. Quality of life was measured by improvement in an index that included data on crime, auto accidents, motor vehicle fatalities, deaths due to other causes, alcoholic beverage consumption, cigarette consumption, unemployment, and pollution.[14]

Improved quality of life in Israel: The quality of life in Israel significantly improved when a large group of TM-Sidhi participants assembled in Jerusalem. In this study, quality of life was measured by an index comprising decreased crime, increased Tel Aviv Stock Exchange Index, and improved national mood (analysis of daily news).[15] Statistically, the possibility of coincidence was less than 1 in 10,000.

Improved international economic trends: During the three-week period of an assembly in which the number of TM-Sidhi participants exceeded the square root of 1% of the world's population, international economic trends improved compared to the combined periods before and after the assembly, as measured by the World Index of International Stock Prices.[16]

Decreased terrorism: During three conferences approaching or exceeding 7,000 participants in the TM-Sidhi program (the square root of 1% of the world's population at the time) there was a significant decrease in fatalities and injuries due to international terrorism. The findings were indicated by time series analysis of an independent data bank.[17]

These studies support the predictions made in the Shiva Samhita and Patanjali Yoga Sutra that the practice of the Transcendental Meditation and TM-Sidhi program, including Yogic Flying, produces a positive, life-supporting effect in the world — it *removes the darkness* in the form of crime, violence, war, and poor quality of life.

The future of world peace

Peace has been the desire of the wise throughout the ages. Many of the greatest minds and most compassionate hearts have tirelessly labored to bring warring nations and unfriendly neighbors together to solve differences, end hostilities, and create amicable relationships. But despite noble intentions and efforts, world peace has been elusive, generation after generation after generation. Clearly, political strategies and diplomatic efforts are inadequate, and are incapable of solving this most pressing problem of human society by themselves.

We now have abundant scientific research documenting the effectiveness of the Transcendental Meditation and TM-Sidhi programs for creating peace. The key lies in collective consciousness. If collective consciousness is filled with stress and hostility, then no amount of diplomacy, regardless of how skillfully applied, will bring a lasting cessation of violence and war. But by creating harmony and coherence in collective consciousness, peace will be automatic and no enemy will be born. In Maharishi's words:

> When one per cent of the world's population practises my Transcendental Meditation technique, or the square root of one per cent of the world's population practises my TM-Sidhi program of Yogic Flying, the entire world consciousness will become coherent. The whole world will become immune to disturbance or disruption of any kind, and world peace will be assured. Every nation will be protected by the almighty, invincible power of Natural Law.[18]

In our next chapter we will examine some long-standing misunderstandings about Yoga, and how they may have emerged from the misinterpretation of Yoga texts.

10
Misunderstandings About Yoga Philosophy

Pure consciousness is an eternal reality, the silent ocean of Being lying at the basis of the ever-changing phenomenal world. It is the immortal ground upon which our ever-expanding universe rests and the creative intelligence within us all. Whether we are aware of it or not, it is always deep inside, always available as our own inner Self.

Throughout the long span of human history the knowledge of Being and how to contact it has been sometimes available but at other times lost to sight. When it has been out of reach, humanity suffers, as both individual and society lose their ability to establish life on its most exalted level.

In time, however, great enlightened teachers, such as Lord Krishna, Buddha, Shankara, and others, have restored the Vedic wisdom in both theory and practice, to provide the experience as well as renew the understanding that direct contact with Being alone can bring fulfillment, peace, and enlightenment. Maharishi speaks of this loss and revival of knowledge as part of a natural cycle of life.[1]

In recent times, this knowledge has been largely lost to view, practiced by a few in remote corners of India and held in its purity by recluses who spent their lives absorbed in the bliss of their own Being. In the middle part of the twentieth century, however, through the inspiration of a great enlightened Indian saint, Brahmananda Saraswati — Maharishi's teacher — this science and technology of consciousness was again brought to light as Maharishi began teaching the Transcendental Meditation technique throughout the world. Though its name reflects a modern terminology, it is as ancient as humankind, suitable for any person in any generation. It has existed throughout time, and brought to light by Maharishi in this age.

In a press conference in 2006, Maharishi explained that "Transcendental Meditation is not my creation. Transcendental Meditation has been throughout the ages, since [time] immemorial," adding that

> People forget about it [Being], someone comes to say it is there within you, he passes away, but this passing away is not of any importance. We do not give importance to the individual, we give importance to the transcendental reality, which transcends the individual and establishes universal, eternal oneness of Being.[2]

In his commentary on the Bhagavad-Gita, Maharishi writes of the loss of the natural experience of Yoga, and how the ensuing search for truth becomes shrouded in effort and strain. Today, an underlying and pervasive teaching is that Yoga — no matter how one defines it — requires hard work as well as perseverance and discipline, and that you will only progress if you have the right attitude, adopt certain beliefs, or try to curb some of your tendencies. To some extent this view reflects the ethic of many modern societies that advocate hard work and discipline as a prerequisite for success, an outlook that has quietly influenced the thinking of modern translators and scholars of Yoga philosophy. Regardless of its origins, though, one apparently cannot escape the assumption that discipline and attitude are fundamental to the development of our inner potential.

Maharishi's view, however, is quite to the contrary. He holds that the path to enlightenment — the path of Yoga — is never difficult. It need not involve arduous discipline and requires only a few minutes a day. And in these few minutes one can unfold Yoga in one's own life, naturally and enjoyably.

If that is so, where did this understanding about effort, strain, and rigorous discipline come from? And of course the all-important follow-up: How do I know that Maharishi's interpretation is correct? In this chapter we will consider a number of common themes in Yoga philosophy and compare Maharishi's comments with the prevailing modern interpretations, and then examine the evidence to see if indeed Maharishi's view holds true.

Concentration

In Chapter 2 we considered the main principles of Transcendental Meditation practice, and discussed how effortlessness is essential for experiencing the state of Yoga — how the mind must become quieter in order to settle into the deep silence of Yoga. And we further saw how an increase in activity, such as one would experience while concentrating, will naturally inhibit the inward dive and keep the awareness bound to the mind's surface. We also learned of the futility of techniques that involve contemplation, at least with respect to experiencing Yoga and developing higher states of consciousness.

How, then, did these meditations become popular, since they seem to obstruct, rather than encourage, the experience of Yoga?

It is difficult to know with certainty how every meditation technique that relies on effort and control evolved, but we can identify persistent themes. Many practices have arisen from confusion between path and goal, which often occurs when someone reads or hears of an account of higher states of consciousness and attempts to emulate it. Perhaps a poet, or ancient Yogi, wrote of an experience of the Self, citing its silence, absence of thoughts, or peaceful nature, and when encountering the description a seeker of enlightenment may have tried to rid the mind of thoughts, hold it in stillness, or imagine the peace.

Let's re-visit a verse from the Upanishads that we examined in Chapter 3 to see how this might work:

सुप्रशान्तः सकृज्ज्योतिः समाधिरचलोऽभयः
Suprashāntaḥ sakṛijjyotiḥ samādhir achalo 'bhayaḥ
(Māṇḍukya Upanishad, 3.37)
[The Self is] deeply peaceful, eternally effulgent, the state of even intelligence, unshakable, and without fear.

This verse presents a compelling and attractive vision, but in the absence of a technique for experiencing the Self someone might try to mentally imitate the description — perhaps by attempting to remain peaceful, calm the mind, maintain a steady state, or perhaps even by imagining the effulgence. In Maharishi's view, however, such practices are ineffective at producing the reality of the inner Self, in part because the effort expended — however slight it might seem — increases mental activity, leading the awareness away from the transcendental experience of the Self. Such attempts will inevitably end in disappointment.

Another example, especially relevant to our consideration of Yoga, occurs in the beginning of the Patanjali Yoga Sutra, in which Yoga is defined:

योगश्चित्तवृत्तिनिरोधः

Yogash chitta-vritti-nirodhaḥ

(Yoga Sutra, 1.2)

A typical translation construes this sutra as: *Yoga is the restriction of the modifications of the mind.*[3] This rendering, along with virtually every other in print, presumes that Yoga in this context refers to the path of Yoga, and thus advocates restricting mental activity — removing thoughts, feelings, creative impulses, etc. Maharishi differs, however, holding that the entire Yoga Sutra is a description of the *state* of Yoga,[4] not the *path*, and that *nirodhaḥ* (*restriction*) does not suggest an intentional inhibition of mental activity. Instead, he translates the sutra as *Yoga is the complete settling of the activity of the mind*, which describes the quiet state of Yoga in which mental activity is naturally at rest.*

Maharishi's point is highly significant, for one who supposes that the sutra describes a path might try to experience Yoga by forcefully inhibiting mental activity. The result, however, will be a more agitated mind, leaving the awareness bound to the surface with little hope of diving deeply within. Similarly, trying to still the mind because Yoga is silent, striving to maintain loving kindness because that is the nature of Yoga, attempting to force the mind to remain in the present, or trying to stare at a candle to make the mind steady, will seldom allow the awareness to settle to quiet levels or bring the mind to Yoga. Such practices, including those found in mindfulness meditations, may have their own value for improving some mental qualities, but to locate the blissful, silent state of Yoga the mind must have a technique for effortlessly becoming less and less active, and ultimately experiencing inner Being.

Eliminating desires

One of the most unfortunate notions associated with modern Yoga practices is that we must control desires — that

---

* Maharishi's translation is consistent with the writings of the great Vedic sage Shankara, who in his commentary on Bhagavad-Gita 6.20 interprets *chittam niruddham* as *chittam uparatim gacchati, the mind becomes quiet*. In this translation, Shankara shows that *niruddham*, derived from the same root as *nirodhah*, does not carry the sense of forcible restriction of the mind, but rather describes a natural state.

we should not enjoy sensory input and should maintain an attitude of equanimity in the face of the so-called pairs of opposites (pleasure and pain, happiness and sorrow, success and failure, etc). The idea is that if we remain balanced in all phases of life — if we control desires and want for nothing — the mind and body will be purified, rendering Yoga more available.

For the most part the concept of controlling or eliminating desires is a byproduct of confusion between path and goal in Yoga texts. Let's consider a verse from the Bhagavad-Gita so that we can better understand how similar expressions have been mistranslated and misconstrued, to the detriment of Yoga aspirants.

This first selection seems to identify desire as an enemy, and one might naturally conclude that progress toward Yoga requires the subjugation of desires.

आवृत्तं ज्ञानमेतेन ज्ञानिनो नित्यवैरिणा
कामरूपेण कौन्तेय दुष्पूरेणानलेन च

*Āvṛittam gyānam etena gyānino nityavairiṇā
kāmarūpeṇa Kaunteya dushpūreṇānalena cha*
(Bhagavad-Gita, 3.39)

Wisdom is veiled by this insatiable flame of desire which is the constant enemy of the wise, O son of Kunti [Arjuna].

Maharishi, however, makes a subtle distinction between the beneficial role of desire and those circumstances in which it is indeed the "constant enemy." He reminds us that desire is natural to life, and impossible to eradicate — and that "any attempt in that direction will only make life dull, useless or tense."[5] He adds:

> Unfortunately it is commonly held that desires should be subdued in order to attain enlightenment. This is completely wrong. The misunderstanding has grown during the last few hundred years, and in consequence the task of those who seek Truth has become more difficult than ever before.[6]

In fact, desire has a crucial role. Our desires constantly propel us toward more and more — more success, happiness, and fulfillment. This tendency for greater happiness enables us to settle deep within during Transcendental Meditation practice, and it also underlies our pursuit of higher states of consciousness. But, as Maharishi further writes, desires may keep us bound to the field of action simply because there is no point in the relative, changing world in which every desire can be satisfied. This can lead to an unending stream of desires for greater happiness that keep us bound to the active world. Maharishi explains:

> This is how the ceaseless activity of desire continues to maintain a close tie of association between the self and the outside world, thus keeping the self bound, as it were, to the field of action.[7]

In this case desire is indeed "the constant enemy of the wise."[8] The solution is to rise above the binding influence of desires, not by forcibly inhibiting them, but by establishing the awareness in Being, the field of pure happiness in which all desires find fulfillment. This alone will allow us to eliminate the harmful effects of desire. To this end, Maharishi explains that Lord Krishna

> is going to give Arjuna a simple technique of transforming the whole machinery that gives rise to desire, of transforming the mind and heart so that the rising up of desires and all their activities will serve as tidal waves of love and bliss in the unbounded ocean of the oneness of God-consciousness. This involves giving a pattern to the machinery that creates desire — senses, mind, and intellect — so that even while remaining in the field of desire, it remains free from the impact of desire.[9]

Lord Krishna's point, then, is not that we should restrict desire, but that we must establish the awareness on that level of life in which all desires find fulfillment. Then those that are helpful and in accord with natural law will continue, and those that are not useful will no longer arise.

This illustrates an important principle of Maharishi's teaching: It is not necessary to destroy darkness to establish light. Rather, one need only bring in the light and the darkness will spontaneously vanish. In other words, it's not necessary to try to control desires — we just bring the awareness to Being, and then unnecessary or harmful desires will naturally disappear.[10]

Remaining unattached

The next verse has a similar theme, concerning itself with avoiding attachment to objects of the senses. It may seem that Lord Krishna is advocating a disciplined approach here, but Maharishi's commentary suggests otherwise.

रागद्वेषवियुक्तैस्तु विषयानिन्द्रियैश्चरन्
आत्मवश्यैर्विधेयात्मा प्रसादमधिगच्छति

Rāga-dwesha-viyuktais tu vishayān indriyaish charan ātmavashyair vidheyātmā prasādam adhigachchhati

(Bhagavad-Gita, 2.64)

But he who is self-disciplined, who moves among the objects of the senses freed from attachment and aversion and under his own control, he attains to "grace."

Maharishi explains that *he who is self-disciplined* refers to one who is established in the Self, established in Cosmic Consciousness, and who lives naturally in a state of self-discipline. Such an individual acts in the field of the senses and experiences their objects, but is not lost among them:

> Maintaining his status in Being he quite naturally maintains evenness of mind. His sense of values is balanced. Acting in the world, he is not lost in it. He is above attachment and detachment, contented in himself, not bound by anything.[11]

The verse does not, therefore, suggest that we should actively discipline ourselves — it advises us to gain freedom from attachment by establishing the awareness in infinite bliss. When we have reached the state of complete fulfillment, in which the Self is experienced as eternally separate from activity, then what experience can create attachment?

Freedom from possessions

There is a sentiment among many seekers of enlightenment that we should not acquire possessions, at least in spirit or attitude — that possessions bind us to the material world, inhibiting Yoga. Few truly believe that we should have no possessions, but there are many who advocate an attitude of minimizing material comforts or objects that we might naturally enjoy.

The following verse apparently supports this interpretation, seemingly suggesting that we give up everything:

निराशीर्यतचित्तात्मा त्यक्तसर्वपरिग्रहः
शारीरं केवलं कर्म कुर्वन्नाप्नोति किल्बिषम्

Nirāshīr yatachittātmā tyakta-sarva-parigrahaḥ
shārīraṃ kevalaṃ karma kurvannāpnoti kilbisham

(Bhagavad-Gita, 4.21)

Expecting nothing, his heart and mind disciplined, having relinquished all possessions, performing action by the body alone, he incurs no sin.

But in Maharishi's view, Lord Krishna is not asking Arjuna to rid himself of possessions. In fact, at the time Lord Krishna was helping him regain his kingdom. Nor was he suggesting that Arjuna adopt a philosophy of not being attached. Maharishi holds that the verse describes transcending, going beyond the material world, and also the experience of Cosmic Consciousness:

> The word "possessions" indicates all that one has gathered around oneself, everything other than one's own Self; relinquishing everything that is outside one's own Self means

> abandoning the whole field of relative existence, being without the three gunas.[12]

In other words, Lord Krishna is recommending that one take the awareness to the transcendental field, which is naturally outside the realm of "all that one has gathered around oneself."

Maharishi's interpretation represents a more literal rendering of the original Sanskrit expression (*tyakta-sarva-parigraha*) than simply *having abandoned all possessions*. *Graha* means *holding* and *pari* refers to *what is all around*, and therefore *parigraha* quite literally pertains to *what is held in the environment by the senses*. Hence, when one transcends one is leaving behind everything (*tyakta-sarva*) that one is engaged with in the relative, material world (*parigraha*).

Performing action by the body alone, he incurs no sin: This, Maharishi explains, refers to the enlightened person, who enjoys a natural state of non-attachment even when engaged in activity:

> The mind of an enlightened man does not register deeply any impressions of actions performed by the body on the level of the senses; through all activities his mind remains ever fixed in Being. Established in the absolute purity of Being, he is out of the field of ignorance, out of the field of 'sin'.[13]

The following verse provides another example. One might construe it as a call for an attitude of non-attachment, but in reality it furnishes us with a vision of life in higher states of consciousness:

यदृच्छालाभसंतुष्टो द्वन्द्वातीतो विमत्सरः
समः सिद्धावसिद्धौ च कृत्वापि न निबध्यते

Yad ṛicchālābhasaṃtushto dwandwātīto vimatsaraḥ
samaḥ siddhāvasiddhau cha kṛitwāpi na nibadhyate

(Bhagavad-Gita, 4.22)

Satisfied with whatever comes unasked, beyond the pairs of opposites, free from envy, balanced in success and failure, even acting he is not bound.

Here we see a picture of a perfectly fulfilled life, untouched by possessions and attachments. One in Cosmic Consciousness spontaneously and permanently lives the transcendental reality, beyond the three gunas, and is therefore naturally *beyond the pairs of opposites*. Envy does not arise, for the enlightened are eternally fulfilled and *balanced in success and failure* — they live in eternal freedom, eternal happiness, but have an unlimited capacity to enjoy life from the platform of non-attachment. This is true freedom.

Maintaining equanimity

The pursuit of equanimity is another theme in Yoga philosophy that has caused significant misunderstanding. Every aspiring Yogi knows that equanimity in all circumstances is a desirable trait. Indeed those who are truly even in any situation are revered for it. Individuals described as saintly or wise often have an unusually calm air about them and are known to "be above" the little commotions of life. The Bhagavad-Gita reveals this quality in the following:

यं हि न व्यथयन्त्येते पुरुषं पुरुषर्षभ
समदुःखसुखं धीरं सोऽमृतत्वाय कल्पते

Yaṃ hi na vyathayantyete puruṣaṃ puruṣarṣabha
Sama-duḥkha-sukhaṃ dhīraṃ so 'mṛitatwāya kalpate
(Bhagavad-Gītā, 2.15)

That man indeed whom these (contacts) do not disturb, who is even-minded in pleasure and pain, steadfast, he is fit for immortality, O best of men!

Contacts refers to contacts of the senses with their objects and implies that whatever comes does not unhinge or upset such individuals, for they are resolute in equanimity.

Commentators have long emphasized the need to cultivate equanimity, in part by renouncing attachments but also by adopting an attitude of calm detachment, of inner serenity. They have suggested that we must, by force of will, grow in tolerance and composure in the face of adversity, and by doing so we will acquire the precious quality of equanimity. It's hard work but worth it, they say. But again Maharishi disagrees:

> At the present time it is generally found that people try to make a mood of equanimity in pleasure and pain, in loss and gain — they try to create a mood of equable behavior and unaffectedness while engaged in the diverse activities of the world. But trying to make a mood on the basis of understanding is simple hypocrisy. Many seekers become trapped in such an attitude.[14]

Maharishi explains that true equanimity grows from establishing the awareness in eternally peaceful, infinitely stable

Being, the state of Yoga. Only then is one truly steadfast in all activities and all circumstances, untouched by problems or difficulties. His comment is important, for it sets the stage for the understanding that life's most urgent need is to dive into the bliss of Yoga. This alone enables us to rise above problems.

The following verse from the Chhandogya Upanishad predicts this very result — that we can rise above suffering and sorrow by establishing our awareness in the Self:

तरति शोकमात्मवित्

Tarati shokam Ātmavit
   (Chhāndogya Upanishad, 7.1.3)
   *Established in the Self, one crosses
   over sorrows and suffering.*[15]

Creating a mood of equanimity or non-attachment, on the other hand, leaves one with nothing other than a mood. It has no bearing on the state of infinite fulfillment, the eternal bliss that spontaneously creates evenness of disposition and eliminates dependence upon anyone or anything.

Renunciation

Sanyasa is a technical term in Yoga philosophy that has been poorly understood by scholars and commentators for some time. Though correctly translated *renunciation*, it has mostly been associated with either the reclusive lifestyle or the attempt to remain indifferent to the results of one's actions.

As a result, the meanings of many important passages in Yoga texts have become distorted and misleading.

In his commentary on the Bhagavad-Gita Maharishi points out that *sanyasa* not only refers to detachment from worldly activities but more broadly to the renunciation of action. The distinction here is significant, because renunciation can mean removing oneself from worldly life — such as living alone in a forest or in a cave — but also the process of going deep within and experiencing the state of Yoga. In this latter sense *sanyasa* describes Transcendental Meditation practice, in which we transcend and experience Yoga, leaving behind all activity and thought. In this state we are truly detached from all aspects of worldly life.[16] Thus when a text suggests *sanyasa* as a means for gaining enlightenment, it may be that it's encouraging us to transcend, to go beyond thought, as a prerequisite for unfolding higher states of consciousness, and not suggesting that we must abandon home and family to dwell in a cave, or that we should become disinterested in the fruits of our activities.

Sanyasa also describes Cosmic Consciousness, in which one experiences the unbounded, infinite Self as separate from activity — one lives infinite freedom, completely independent of the surrounding world. In the following passage, Maharishi explains this point:

> When, by the practice of Karma Yoga — the practice of Transcendental Meditation supplemented by activity — one begins to live Being together with activity, one experiences

> It [the Self] as separate from activity, and this experience of separation of one's Self from activity is called renunciation. Renunciation is thus gained automatically through the practice of Yoga.[17]

Unity Consciousness, the most mature state of Yoga, is also *sanyasa*, because one experiences the entire relative world as an expression of one's own Self, thereby enjoying the most complete, most fully developed freedom from worldly activity.

These states, whether enjoyed by a person of the world or by a recluse, are more profound values of renunciation than the simple life removed from day-to-day activities. Shankara, one of the enlightened members of the tradition of Vedic teachers, spoke extensively of *sanyasa* in the context of the reclusive lifestyle as well as the need for transcending and living higher states of consciousness. Unfortunately, translators and commentators have neglected the latter, thus distorting the proper understanding of his teaching.

Self-remembering

Self-remembering is a technique in which one attempts to remain engaged in the outer environment while also maintaining awareness of the Self within. This type of practice may have originated from a spontaneous glimpse of Cosmic Consciousness — an experience of the infinite Self along with the activities of life. Such experiences sometimes come naturally and unbidden to individuals born with refined nervous systems, and the practice of self-remembering appears to be an understandable attempt to regain them. As with many practices, it seems to have arisen from a confusion between path and goal.

With no disrespect to those who have employed and taught self-remembering, from Maharishi's perspective trying to remember the inner Self while engaged in the outer world will not bring one to Yoga, and is therefore not useful for cultivating higher states of consciousness. If anything, trying to do two things at once will divide the mind and may make it weaker.

Whose interpretation should I believe?
In this chapter we have examined Maharishi's comments on several aspects of Yoga philosophy, in particular some of the practices employed in the name of Yoga. Maharishi's disagreement with many of the most common modern interpretations of the core texts of Yoga philosophy leads us to an interesting challenge: Whom should we believe? It's a fair question, and though Maharishi's logic appears sound, his conclusions are unique, and therefore we must consider them carefully.

For the most part, the differences can be reduced to a few simple issues, not the least of which is the role of effort in Yoga practice. Modern meditation practices generally require some kind of effort — concentration or discipline — and frequently advocate changes in attitude and behavior.

Maharishi, on the other hand, holds that concentration, effort, etc., are founded upon mistaken understandings that have insinuated themselves into Yoga philosophy. A proper path to Yoga, he feels, must be effortless, natural, and simple. And there is no need to alter attitudes or behaviors, as these will change appropriately as consciousness grows. In this view, practicing the Transcendental Meditation technique twice a day, comfortably and enjoyably, is enough to promote action fully in accord with dharma, natural law, as we saw in Chapter 6.

The simplest way to decide is to evaluate the results — what works. From the earliest days of his teaching, Maharishi understood that we live in a scientific age, and that even reports of the most sublime experiences will inevitably encounter some skepticism unless supported by empirical evidence. He knew that the benefits of his program were real and concrete, but he also saw how the concept of meditation had been shrouded in mysticism, resulting in the sentiment that it wasn't for the practically-minded. He therefore emphasized scientific verification, and challenged scientists from all over the world to test the effects of his meditation. The result has been a rich resource of empirical evidence.

Scientific research supporting Maharishi's interpretation
Research on the Transcendental Meditation program has been relatively easy in some respects, because there are over

seven million practitioners worldwide, many of whom have been meditating twice a day for thirty, forty years or more. That alone is revealing, for few would persist for so long if the outcomes were not satisfying. But more to the point, researchers have had an abundance of subjects for both short- and long-term studies, all practicing the identical procedure taught in the same systematic way throughout the world. In the following sections, we'll examine some of the research on the Transcendental Meditation program as it pertains to different modern understandings of Yoga philosophy and Yoga practice.

Concentration

In Chapter 2 we discussed research concerning the effects of different meditations on the brain. There we encountered a wide variety of meditations, all of which produce EEG signatures characteristic of more active brain physiologies. This is not surprising, insofar as these techniques require some kind of effort and/or concentration. While such practices have their own benefits, they do not promote the experience of Yoga. So far, only the Transcendental Meditation program has been shown to produce the global coherent alpha waves associated with the experience of pure consciousness, the state of Yoga.

More appropriate desires, better choices

Should one restrict those desires that are not useful for the growth of consciousness — that are not helpful to life? Is desire an enemy that needs to be conquered? Maharishi writes that unhealthy desires will naturally fall away with regular Transcendental Meditation practice, and that better behavior is not a means to Yoga but rather a spontaneous byproduct.

Below are a few studies that support Maharishi's point. As you'll see, these show the growth of healthier behavior in a variety of ways, a variety of settings, and with a variety of subjects:

Moral reasoning: According to the psychologist Lawrence Kohlberg, there are six clearly defined stages of moral development. As one moves through the stages, one becomes better able to respond more appropriately to moral dilemmas. In a study that examined the relationship between Transcendental Meditation practice and Kohlberg's stages of moral reasoning, meditating university students showed significantly higher levels of moral maturity in comparison to control students who were about to learn. The controls displayed the same level as those who were not planning to learn, indicating that the observed difference among the meditating participants was due to changes that occurred after instruction.[18]

Improved behavior: In a study on adolescent children with high normal systolic blood pressure, researchers found that the students who took the Transcendental Meditation course showed significant decreases in absenteeism, school rule infractions, and in suspension days, after just four months of practice.[19] On a similar note, prison inmates — who display a high level of inappropriate behavior — demonstrated many positive changes as a result of their Transcendental Meditation practice, including decreased negativism, decreased resentment, and decreased suspicion,[20] as well as decreased aggression,[21] decreased verbal hostility,[22] and an increase in experiences of higher states of consciousness.[23]

Better choices: Drug and alcohol abuse is also symptomatic of poor decision-making and inappropriate desires. In independent studies, individuals demonstrated a decreased use of alcohol, cigarettes, and illegal drugs, indicating more positive desires in the direction of health and progress.[24] Similarly, a study of executives and workers in the automotive industry found that after three months of regular practice, participants in a Transcendental Meditation course showed decreased cigarette and liquor consumption, in comparison to controls from the same work sites.[25]

Healthier lifestyle: The above studies show a decrease in the use of damaging substances, but often the improvements are found in the desire for more healthy lifestyle practices. For example, managers at a medical equipment company who took the Transcendental Meditation course showed more healthy behavior after three months of practice, as measured by reduced alcohol consumption and more healthy and regular habits of exercise, diet, and sleep.[26]

And again, when learning the Transcendental Meditation program one is not taught about behavior — the instructors never tell the students how to act, what to do, which choices are more life-supporting, and which are life-damaging. They teach a simple mental technique and the behavioral benefits emerge naturally, always in a positive direction.

Reduced attachment

Practitioners of the Transcendental Meditation program also grow in independence and self-sufficiency, both measures of growing freedom from attachment. There are a number of ways to measure changes in these qualities, including the assessment of levels of happiness and satisfaction, equanimity, and flexibility — the willingness to relinquish previously held attitudes and conceptions, along with receptivity to the opinions, positions, and attitudes of others.

In the study from the automotive industry cited earlier, researchers found increased job satisfaction as well as increased professional and personal satisfaction after three months of Transcendental Meditation practice, as compared to controls from the same work sites.[27] This growth of inner contentment is essentially a symptom of a natural state of non-attachment, in which fulfillment comes from the experience of happiness within and the consequent equanimity during the ups and downs of life. In a similar study, employees who learned the Transcendental Meditation program showed a significant growth of happiness and satisfaction in life in comparison to control subjects, as reflected in their decreased desire to change jobs.[28]

Sometimes a work environment can be highly stressful, and even though many may love their jobs and strive toward higher of performance, they can nonetheless be burdened by the stressful environment with its attendant long- and short-term health difficulties. In a study performed at a high-security government agency, which was reported to be extremely stressful, those who took the Transcendental Meditation course displayed decreased depression in comparison to control employees who participated in an educational stress-management program. After three years the meditating employees continued to show significant reductions in depression.[29] This demonstrates an improved ability to function independently of the deleterious aspects of the work environment.

Rigid thinking and closed-mindedness can also be signs of excessive attachment — one tends to hold onto ideas and perspectives regardless of their contextual suitability. In one study, a researcher found that practitioners of the Transcendental Meditation technique were significantly more open-minded than both prospective meditators and a non-meditating control group. The use of prospective practitioners answers the criticism that those who learn the Transcendental Meditation program are naturally more open-minded.[30] Similarly, after fourteen weeks of Transcendental Meditation practice, secondary students showed increased tolerance, in contrast to control students.[31]

Couples introduced to the Transcendental Meditation technique showed an increased ability to be objective, fair-minded, and reasonable.[32] Again, the growth of these qualities indicates improvement in the direction of non-attachment — the ability to hold less rigidly to thoughts, ideas, and perspectives.

Equanimity

A number of studies have found that practitioners of the Transcendental Meditation program are more balanced in their outlook, less likely to become upset with difficulties, and more calm and patient. Among the specific findings, each of which contributes uniquely to a more balanced and even state of mind, are decreased depression,[33] increased self-esteem,[34] increased self-concept,[35] increased self-actualization,[36] decreased trait anxiety, decreased job tension, improved work and personal relationships,[37] decreased anxiety,[38] increased job satisfaction, improved relationships with co-workers, and improved relationships with supervisors.[39]

Even maximum security inmates who learned the Transcendental Meditation technique demonstrated spontaneous growth of equanimity, as measured by decreased negativism, decreased resentment, decreased suspicion, decreased tendency to assault, and decreased verbal hostility,[40] as well as decreased aggression.[41]

In this chapter we have examined several aspects of Yoga philosophy that, in Maharishi's view, have been misunderstood in recent centuries. In the next chapter we will consider Ashtanga Yoga, a central component of Yoga philosophy first brought to light in the Patanjali Yoga Sutra.

11
Ashtanga Yoga: The Eight Limbs of Yoga

Ashtanga Yoga is a popular system introduced to the modern world by K. Pattabhi Jois, a twentieth century Indian Yoga teacher. Though it has a number of variations, it is principally taught today as the synchronizing of breath with a series of Yoga postures to cleanse the muscles and organs. It often includes internal and external practices for purifying mind, body, and behavior.

Most teachers, including Jois, cite the Patanjali Yoga Sutra as the authority for their practices, and indeed it is the first Yoga text to employ the term *Ashtanga Yoga*. *Ashta* in Sanskrit means *eight* and *anga* means *limb*, and thus the most common translation of *Ashtanga Yoga* is *the eight limbs of Yoga*.

Modern Yoga teachers in this system almost universally describe the eight limbs as eight steps of purification that are prerequisites to experiencing Yoga, however they define Yoga. In this view, the first four limbs — *yama*, *niyama*, *asana*, and *pranayama* — are regarded as external cleansing practices, while the next three — *pratyahara*, *dharana*, and *dhyan* — are seen as practices for cleansing the inner person. *Samadhi* is said to be the Yogic state, attainable after sufficient purification. Teachers who advocate practicing these eight limbs differ on whether they should be employed in a strict sequence or whether they can be applied where and as needed according to a student's progress and development.

Maharishi's commentary on the Patanjali Yoga Sutra

Maharishi, not surprisingly, has quite a different interpretation. In his view, the Yoga Sutra does not advocate a practice called Ashtanga Yoga, rather it describes the state of Yoga, especially in its most mature level of Unity Consciousness. Ashtanga Yoga is, in Maharishi's account, a detailed and comprehensive description of the eight fundamental characteristics of the state of Yoga. In his words:

> [The Yoga Sutra] does not suggest any practice because it's a philosophy, it is an understanding about life, an understanding of complete life. It is the description of the goal, even though the descriptions can have good meanings to describe the path as well.[1]

Maharishi here distinguishes between the use of the technical terminology of Yoga in the Yoga Sutra and in other Yoga texts. While terms such as *pranayama* and *asana* refer to Yoga practices in much of the literature, the Yoga Sutra ascribes to them a more fundamental understanding as qualities of intelligence, or characteristics, of the state of Unity.

Thus the delineation of Ashtanga Yoga in the Yoga Sutra is not a how-to manual, as is often thought, but rather a philosophical description of different characteristics of the state of Yoga. In this view, the eight limbs are not techniques, but rather are qualities of Yoga, which taken together reveal its comprehensive structure.²

Maharishi's interpretation is critical for a proper understanding of Yoga philosophy. Take the five *yamas*, for example. Trying to observe *satya* (truth) is a noble aspiration, as is endeavoring to practice *ahimsa* (non-violence). But it is misleading to say that doing either will bring you to the state of Yoga. For that you have to transcend. Trying to be more truthful or act with less violence will not facilitate diving deep within and experiencing pure consciousness, and without that experience it will be difficult to rise to higher states of consciousness.

The eight limbs of Yoga

Maharishi's commentary begins with an analysis of the term Ashtanga Yoga. He points out that *ashtanga* (*ashta* + *anga*) is Sanskrit for *eight limbs*, not *eight steps*, and that Ashtanga Yoga cannot, therefore, be a series of steps for reaching Yoga. He further reasons that limbs are by nature extensions, and that just as limbs grow with a body's development, the eight limbs are aspects of Yoga that grow as Yoga unfolds.

> The limbs of a body grow all together. If one limb grows, the other grows. All eight limbs grow: They keep on growing and growing and growing, until each of them has grown to the fullest value, and the body is fully developed.³

In other words, *satya*, *truth*, develops spontaneously as Yoga grows in our life. Likewise *ahimsa*, *non-violence* grows automatically as the body of Yoga unfolds. They are not steps to gain Yoga, but are part of the very structure of Yoga, which develop automatically with Yoga grows.

Maharishi further comments that these limbs constitute the body of Yoga, and that in order to understand Yoga we must consider the limbs.

> It is these eight limbs that constitute the state of Yoga, the body of Yoga, and the consideration of these eight limbs gives us the comprehensive structure of Yoga. Yoga sutras, the aphorisms of Yoga, are to bring the total knowledge of Yoga. To bring the total knowledge of Yoga, certain things must be considered. Patanjali rises to consider these eight fields of life and declares that the body of Yoga, the state of life in integration, or unity, is composed of these eight limbs.[4]

With this perspective in mind, let's examine Maharishi's comments on the different limbs, so that we can understand how each comprises an aspect of the state of Yoga.

The eight limbs are:

1. *yama* — the administrator, which administers the eight aspects of Yoga and keeps them bound together
2. *niyama* — laws through which the administrator governs
3. *asana* — the seat, or stability, of Unity
4. *pranayama* — the movement, the impulse of activity
5. *pratyahara* — experiences that satisfies the senses
6. *dharana* — holding on to Unity
7. *dhyan* — meditation
8. *samadhi* — Transcendental Consciousness, the union of individual awareness with cosmic intelligence

1. Yama

The first limb of Yoga is *yama*, derived from the Sanskrit *yam* meaning *to uphold* or *to support*. *Yama* is often translated as *self-control* or *self-restraint*, and is thought to be a system of behavioral purification. The idea is that by practicing the five *yamas* (below) one will improve interactions with others and with the environment, thus setting the stage for either the experience or practice of Yoga (depending upon who is interpreting).

Maharishi, however, describes yama as the quality of intelligence that is the administrator, which administers the eight aspects of Yoga and keeps them bound together in the body of Yoga. These dynamics maintain the integrated state of Unity, in which individual life and cosmic life are lived as one (see Chapter 7). Maharishi goes on to describe yama as the field of Cosmic Law — universal, eternal Being.

> Yama, the administrator, is everywhere. Take up anything and you will find its structure in such a beautiful, systematic way — the present structure and its evolutionary process into all possible future structures. There must be some administrator there. [The Yoga Sutra] describes what that administrator is when [it] details what Yama is — that which is the administrator of the body of Yoga.[5]

Yama rules through its five aspects, five administrators that keep the limbs together. These are known as the five yamas.

The five yamas
The five aspects of yama are:

i. *satya* — truth that never changes
ii. *ahimsa* — non-injury, non-harm
iii. *asteya* — non-stealing
iv. *brahmacharya* — living alone, living Brahm
v. *aparigraha* — non-accumulation

Yoga teachers often suggest that one practice speaking the truth (satya); not injuring anyone or anything in thought, word, or deed (ahimsa); not taking what belongs to others (asteya); celibacy (brahmacharya); and controlling greedy tendencies (aparigraha). The assumption is that by following such a course the student will purify behavior, live a better life, and become qualified for other practices such as meditation.

Maharishi, however, notes again that in the Yoga Sutra these are not steps — they are characteristics of the state of Yoga that spontaneously and automatically grow as Yoga develops.

The following is a brief analysis of each from Maharishi's perspective:

i. Satya

Satya generally means *truth*, but every Sanskrit word has many layers of meaning and it's not necessarily appropriate to apply the same meaning for each context. Maharishi describes *satya* on its most fundamental level as *that which never changes*, and in Ashtanga Yoga it is the "non-changeability, stability, infinity, immortality, that is the first symptom of the administrator."[6] In other words, a principal characteristic of the administrator is that it is immortal, non-changing, infinite. It is pure consciousness, Being, the level of life that knows no change.

In the following quote, Maharishi discusses the nature of truth, and how only eternal, unchanging Being can be considered truth:

> The truth is what? That which never changes. What is that which never changes? Being alone is that which never changes. Being is samadhi. [The Yoga Sutra] puts samadhi as the eighth limb of the body of Yoga, but puts satya, Being, right in the beginning. This means that the state of Yoga is Being at its beginning and Being at its end. Being is all permeating and this is the state of Yoga, the state of union.[7]

Maharishi further explains that if we want to speak the truth, we must first develop our consciousness:

> Speaking truth cannot be practiced. What can be practiced is the development of that level of consciousness which will always speak truth. If speaking truth has to be practiced, it has to be practiced in the developing value of pure consciousness. If that level of consciousness is not there one can't speak truth; there will be some lack of truth.[8]

Maharishi makes a subtle, but important, clarification. We always speak from the level of our own consciousness. If consciousness is not fully developed, then we can never be assured of speaking truth. On the other hand, our capacity to speak truth spontaneously grows as a result of developing consciousness through the experience of Yoga.

As consciousness expands, we naturally grow in speaking truth because we are acting more and more in accord with natural law.*

ii. Ahimsa

Ahimsa, or *non-harm*, was a singular element of the philosophy of Mahatma Gandhi, the non-violent revolutionary who helped free India from British rule in the middle of the 20th century. Gandhi was deeply committed to never harming anything regardless of the physical danger that might come to him.

Gandhi's understanding of ahimsa was not incorrect, for in the context of his work ahimsa refers to a non-violent approach to life. But the Yoga Sutra reveals a deeper understanding of ahimsa, as a quality, or characteristic, of Unity.

Unity includes everything — there is nothing outside it. Therefore, if everything is experienced as an expression of one's Self, there is nothing to give offence to nor to receive offence from — there is no harm anywhere. Maharishi explains:

> Unity, because it is Unity — a state of non-difference — doesn't have anything else to fight. Immortality knows no mortality. Infinity knows no finite. Stability knows no change. Unity knows no difference. And therefore, Unity is a state absolutely devoid of any possibility of offence. There is nothing [that is] "other." The state of Unity is devoid of

---

* See Chapter 6: Yoga and Dharma.

difference, and therefore there is no other, and therefore the natural state of non-violence is in the structure of Unity.[9]

This quality of non-violence naturally grows in our life from the regular experience of Yoga. As one continues practicing the Transcendental Meditation technique, non-harm becomes spontaneously evident in all aspects of life, as Maharishi explains:

> The state of non-violence is a level of consciousness in which one always produces life-supporting influence, a state of life in which life-damaging influence can simply not be created. That is that state in Cosmic Consciousness where awareness is unbounded and one is just a witness to everything — one's whole aspiration of life, one's whole impulse of life, is conducted by cosmic intelligence, and then every step of action is for evolution.[10]

Maharishi clarifies here that true ahimsa comes from unfolding one's own consciousness, because ahimsa is a natural characteristic of Yoga. Though the practice of non-injury is certainly laudable, it is not a means to experience Yoga — we must transcend to accomplish that. But when one establishes the awareness in Yoga, then non-violence grows naturally and spontaneously.

iii. Asteya

Asteya means *to not commit theft* — to not take someone else's property. In this context, the Yoga Sutra is defining an aspect of *yama*, the administrator, which we can better understand by reviewing our understanding of Cosmic Consciousness.

In Cosmic Consciousness one experiences unbounded awareness together with the waking state. The two levels are simultaneous but independent, in the sense that one appreciates the boundaries of perception while concurrently experiencing the infinite Self. Prior to Cosmic Consciousness, however, it is a different story — our experience is dominated by objective phenomena, while the true nature of the Self is concealed. For example, when looking at a rose all that remains in the awareness is the rose — the true nature of the infinite, unbounded Self is as though hidden. In Maharishi's words:

> The essential nature of the subject or the experiencer within is lost in the experience of the object, just as though the object had annihilated the subject, and the subject misses the experience of its own essential nature while engaged in the experience of the object. Only the object remains in the consciousness. This is what the common experience of people is.[11]

On the other hand, when one is enjoying Cosmic Consciousness, the perception of the rose no longer overshadows the Self — one appreciates the rose along with the experience of infinite, unbounded Being. One no longer "possesses" the rose, and the rose no longer "possesses" the Self. This, Maharishi feels, is the deepest significance of asteya — the awareness is no longer overshadowed and is therefore not "possessing" the object, it witnesses it. Maharishi explains:[12]

> When the self has gained the ability to maintain unboundedness and is also capable of maintaining the boundaries of perception, then the object of perception has been "thrown off," and then the self does not "possess" the object. This is "not-possessing the flower."[13]

The situation is different in Unity Consciousness, because everything is perceived in terms of the Self:

> In this state, the possession of the flower is not the possession of something that one does not own. The flower is in the value of the Self, and therefore the Self belongs to the flower. The flower belongs to the Self, and in this sense the flower is no longer different from the Self. Therefore the Self owns the flower completely.[14]

Thus in Unity Consciousness, the Self completely possesses the rose. One experiences the rose as an expression of one's own Self, and therefore "owns" it.

iv. Brahmacharya

Brahmacharya means *celibacy* — living a life alone, unmarried. But in Ashtanga Yoga there is a different sense of the term, which Maharishi explains as follows: "*Charya* means *living*. *Brahmacharya* means *living Brahman*. Living Brahman [Brahm] means living the supremely elevated state of consciousness. That's all, simple. Living Unity."[15] It's important to note, though, that Maharishi frequently emphasizes that the Transcendental Meditation technique is for everyone, whether they live in a family or choose to live alone.

v. Aparigraha

Aparigraha means *non-accumulation*, and is usually interpreted as *renouncing possessions* or *controlling greed*. But in Maharishi's view, *aparigraha* describes life in Unity Consciousness, in which everything is found in terms of the Self:

> Because when everything is in terms of myself, when everything is in terms of infinity, then everything is as good as myself. Only then is the state naturally developed in which one does not accumulate many things, because if there is accumulation, it is the accumulation of the Self, by the Self, for the Self, in the Self; and Self and Self means nothing is separate. Therefore, in the state of Unity the quality of non-accumulation is spontaneously available.[16]

Maharishi's point is that one in Unity Consciousness is naturally without possessions, because everything is experienced as an expression of one's own Self — there is no "other," for even the food one eats and the clothes one wears are just oneself in the appearance of food and clothes. It's just a simple state of life. In Transcendental Consciousness as well there are no possessions — one has transcended the world, and there is nothing in this state of Yoga that is not the Self. One *is* the infinite ocean of unbounded, pure wakefulness, and nothing else.

2. Niyama

Niyama means *law*, usually referring to rules or observances. In the Yoga Sutra, it refers to those laws, those principles, through which Yama functions, which together uphold the structure of Unity. Maharishi notes that *ni* in Sanskrit means *to lead*, and therefore these laws lead yama — the administrator governs through these laws.

The five niyamas are:
i *shaucha* — purity
ii *santosha* — contentment
iii *tapas* — increasing glow of life
iv *swadhyaya* — opening to the chapter of the Self
v *Ishwara-pranidhan* — opening the awareness to the maintainer of the universe

i. Shaucha

Shaucha means *purity*, a fundamental characteristic of Yoga. The experience of Yoga in Transcendental Consciousness is beyond time and space, and therefore by definition is completely pure and unsullied by outside influences. Nothing can stain it, change it, or make it impure. Similarly, one in Unity Consciousness enjoys the most mature state of Yoga, which cannot be touched or made impure. In Unity Consciousness one lives and breathes cosmic life, and there are no outside influences since everything is in terms of the Self.

Maharishi further explains that experiencing this field of purity is the only effective way to increase purity in life, because stresses in the nervous system — the structural or material abnormalities that inhibit proper physiological functioning — constrain the unfoldment of pure consciousness and prevent real, lasting purity. Attempts to increase purity through attitude changes and resolutions may have some small effect, but they do not facilitate the release of stress from the nervous system and thus do not help us experience pure consciousness. It is profound rest, which we gain during Transcendental Meditation practice, that enables the nervous system to grow in true purity, as Maharishi explains:

> There is no way to gain purity other than by releasing stresses and gaining purity of the nervous system. A mood does not have the slightest power to transform body and mind.[17]

Maharishi's point is that a resolution to be pure will not bring purity to the nervous system. Real purity arises from developing higher states of consciousness.

This view is well-supported by scientific research. In Chapter 7 we saw how the qualities inherent within pure consciousness — such as peace, creativity, happiness, and purity — spontaneously grow as a result of the regular experience of the inner Self. In Chapters 5 and 6 we saw how the body naturally becomes more healthy and behavior spontaneously improves from regular practice of the Transcendental Meditation technique. Regular practice even results in a natural propensity to avoid damaging influences, such as cigarettes, alcohol, and recreational drugs, also indicating greater purity in life.

ii. Santosha

Santosha means *contentment*. In Maharishi's account contentment can be achieved by living infinity — living the infinite, eternal, unbounded level of life.

> The only way to make this second law of structuring Unity [Santosha, contentment] a living reality of our daily life is to gain affluence, and we really start to gain affluence from the level of Transcendental Consciousness. The subjective value of affluence becomes permanent in Cosmic Consciousness and the objective value reaches supreme relative value in God Consciousness. 200% of affluence — 100% on the level of the objective value of life and 100% on the level of the subjective value of life, total contentment, complete fulfillment — is gained in the state of Unity alone.[18]

Here again we encounter Maharishi's theme that the description of a state of consciousness is not the path. In this case, trying to become content will not bring one to Yoga. It's the other way around — only the experience of Yoga will bring true and lasting contentment.

iii. Tapas

If you read books or peruse web sites on Ashtanga Yoga, you'll often find *tapas* translated as *austerity*, usually in the sense of abstaining from the joys of life, from sensory experience, in order to attain Yoga. Some also feel that it refers to willingly enduring hardships as a means of purifying mind and body. In many cases *austerity* is softened to simply *discipline*.

According to Maharishi, this understanding is wrong and potentially damaging. In his view, tapas is a natural quality that spontaneously increases as one becomes more and more familiar with Transcendental Consciousness.

> The actual word meaning of *tapas* is *heating* — increasing in glow of life. Life is infinity, immortality, immovability, unboundedness, absolute, and so the increasing value of the glow of life means increasing value of infinity, of immortality, of unboundedness, of absolute Being.[19]

Tapas is available only as purity grows through experiencing Yoga and developing one's consciousness. As Maharishi emphasizes, making a mood of austerity has nothing to do with the experience of Yoga.

iv. Swadhyaya

The fourth niyama is called *swadhyaya*. *Swa* refers to the *Self*, *adhyaya* means *chapter*, and so *swadhyaya* can be rendered *opening to the chapter of the Self* or *the awareness opening to the Self*.[20] The use of chapter is deliberate and precise, Maharishi feels, because it explains the experience of moving from one state to another. During Transcendental Meditation practice, "opening our awareness to the Self is experienced in the sense of opening a new chapter."[21] It is as though one chapter (waking state awareness) closes and Transcendental Consciousness opens. Similarly, we close the chapter of Cosmic Consciousness as we grow into God Consciousness, and likewise for the unfoldment of Unity Consciousness from God Consciousness. As Maharishi puts it, "this chapter gets completely closed, that chapter opens. This side closes, that side opens."[22]

v. Ishwara-pranidhan

Ishwara means *governor* or *maintainer* — one who governs life, who maintains creation. *Pranidhan* refers to *bringing that level of life to our consciousness, to our life*. Thus *Ishwara-pranidhan* is the quality of *opening our awareness to the maintainer*.[23]

Maharishi describes two maintainers: One is pure Being, the maintainer of the absolute, non-changing transcendental level of life; the second is the very finest level of creation from which all the laws of nature organize and administer. The latter is the maintainer of the universe. Maharishi refers to this level as celestial, and explains that God Consciousness brings a state of oneness with the celestial level of life. Thus,

> *Pranidhan* means *imbibing in our Self* — completely opening ourself to that value of the finest relative and the Absolute. This is Ishwara-pranidhan. This is surrendering ourself. When we talk of surrender, the first supreme value of the surrender that comes is oneness of our awareness with the finest relative, supremely celestial value of life.[24]

In this way, Ishwara-pranidhan describes a characteristic quality of Yoga in Transcendental Consciousness, but also in the maturation of Yoga in Cosmic Consciousness, in God Consciousness, and finally in Unity Consciousness.

3. Asana

Asana is the third of the five *yamas*. It means *seat* and often refers to the physical postures of Yoga exercise. When people go to a studio for Yoga they generally practice asanas, many of which Maharishi prescribed as a preparation for meditation. But the Yoga Sutra describes a more fundamental value of asana: It is the seat, the stability, of Unity.

> [The Yoga Sutra] describes the stable aspect, the stability of Yoga. Where is this stability of Yoga? Naturally on the level of the body; naturally on the level of the mind; naturally on the level of senses; naturally on the level of intellect; naturally on the level of Being; naturally on the level of the environment; naturally on the level of the whole universe. It is in the midst of all differences, because union is non-difference, and the state of non-difference is everywhere.[25]

Maharishi explains stability as a feature of Yoga on every level: it is a quality of consciousness, but also of mind and body. On the transcendental level, the Self is not subject to ups and downs, to invasion from the outside, because there is nothing outside it. It is immovable, impermeable, infinitely stable.

In the same way, Unity Consciousness has nothing outside it, nothing to damage, stain, or diminish it. To experience Unity one must be stable — the nervous system must be strong, flexible, and capable of maintaining infinite, unbounded awareness, infinite silence, in the midst of dynamic activity. This strength and stability includes every level of life because Unity is maintained in the midst of all differences.

4. Pranayama

The fourth limb is *pranayama*. With respect to Yoga practice *pranayama* refers to breathing exercises that refine the physiology and settle the mind. Maharishi advocates specific pranayama techniques as preparation for meditation. In the context of Ashtanga Yoga, however, Maharishi locates a deeper understanding.

Maharishi explains *prana* as the basic force of life responsible for all activity throughout the universe. In the context of the Yoga Sutra, it is the force that enlivens each of the eight limbs individually while also keeping them bound together. In explaining this point he notes that prana inspires the activity of each individual cell in the body while simultaneously maintaining the connectedness of all the cells.[26] In the same way, prana enlivens each of the eight limbs of Yoga individually while simultaneously keeping them bound in Unity.

> Prana is the life force, the basic cause of all activity. It enlivens these eight different values of life, and then puts them together, as if harmonizing them. And in the collective form, prana makes them all breathe one breath of Unity, and that is unity of life.[27]

Maharishi further explains that the connection between individuality and universality — the connection between individual and cosmic intelligence — is established by action, and thus without prana, the basic cause of all activity, this connection cannot exist. If this connection did not exist, there would be no experience of Yoga:

> Without the basic force of activity, without prana, no connection between individuality and universality is possible. Without that basic force of life, the impulse of activity, these different limbs will not come to be joined together. It is the force of prana, it is the life force, that infuses breath — that enlivens these eight limbs while at the same time putting them together.[28]

Ayama means *coming and going*, and thus in this context pranayama is the movement, the impulse, of activity.

5. Pratyahara

Ahara means *food*, and *prati* gives the sense of reversing direction. Thus *pratyahara* (*prati* + *ahara*) means something like *food from the inverse direction*, or *food from the opposite direction*.[29]

In the Yoga Sutra, Maharishi explains, food refers to anything that nourishes or satisfies the senses, and therefore in Ashtanga Yoga pratyahara relates to the direction in which the senses are more fulfilled. We've seen that it is the nature of life to always move in the direction of greater charm, greater enjoyment, and if unrestricted the mind and senses will always move from a less to a more enjoyable experience.

Modern practitioners and teachers of Ashtanga Yoga often interpret pratyahara as the need to turn the senses inward, the idea being that the outer world is superficial and of limited value, and one wishing to experience Yoga should turn the attention away from it. According to this interpretation, once one has mastered forcing the attention inward, then one will be better equipped to experience Yoga.

Maharishi differs, however, for in his view "food" is found wherever the senses naturally gain satisfaction. He explains:

> In whatever direction satisfaction is found, that is the natural direction of the senses. In that direction they are found to travel — inward, outward, left, right, up, down. Doesn't matter what direction, but the direction of the senses is toward where they get food — perception, experience — and food is that which satisfies.[30]

Maharishi's point, then, is that pratyahara refers to experience that satisfies the senses regardless of where it is found. But he adds that the experience during Transcendental Meditation practice is characterized by increasing charm. The finer phase of objective existence is more charming and thus when given the opportunity the senses naturally move toward it.

This is the experience of Transcendental Meditation practitioners, who find that the senses are directed inwards during meditation without effort or control. The reason is that the inward direction is simply more fulfilling. But the awareness cannot be forced — satisfaction comes naturally through the principle of increasing charm. Thus, in Maharishi's view, interpreting pratyahara as a practice for forcing the senses to change their direction would be counter to Patanjali's inspiration of establishing the field of the senses as one of the eight areas of consideration.

6. Dharana

Dharana means *holding* or *grasping*. What is holding and what is being held? A fundamental characteristic of higher states of consciousness is the mind's ability to "hold onto" absolute Being while remaining engaged in dynamic activity — not through force but because at that level the mind is fully established in Being. In Maharishi's words:

> In this state of Yoga mind holds, upholds Being. The mind held *by* Being, the mind held *in* Being — whatever we say, whether "in being" or "by being," it doesn't matter. The mind held in Being is the holding that [the Yoga Sutra describes] as the sixth limb of Yoga.[31]

This quality of holding is not only applicable to the field of the mind, but to every limb of Yoga, to every aspect of Yoga, to the whole field of Yoga, because "it is by this holding that the state of Yoga is sustained."[32]

7. Dhyan

The closest English equivalent to *dhyan* is *meditation*, which Maharishi describes as "a deeper value of holding." He explains that *dharana* sustains or maintains, whereas *dhyan* is the process underlying *dharana*.

The main difference between them is that *dharana* corresponds to the mind — the aspect of our mental functions that thinks — whereas *dhyan* corresponds to the intellect, the discriminative aspect of mental functioning. We can better understand the distinction between mind and intellect — and therefore between *dharana* and *dhyan* — through an example.

Imagine going to a store to purchase a flower. The mental impulse that thinks and moves around is said to be the mind, but the quality of our subjectivity that decides "I want this flower instead of that one" is a function of what we call the intellect. The intellect discriminates, decides, while the mind thinks. Maharishi explains:

> What is the impulse that starts to shift from one to the other, says no to this, says yes to this? It is that silent, quiet phase of our inner life which we call intellect. It is the intellect which quietly decides, discriminates. And the quiet discriminative value of the intellect is vivid on the level of the mind. The mind thinks. It jumps from one field to the other, but the impulse to shift from one to the other is the intellect, the deciding value. That which functions is the mind.[33]

So the mind belongs to *dharana* because it holds all our experiences and therefore holds the transcendental Absolute in the state of Yoga. This is *dharana*. In Maharishi's account, however, transcending belongs to the intellect, because the intellect decides to move from the gross level of thought to a more refined level — it recognizes that each subtler impulse of thought is more charming and decides to go with that more pleasing value. It is automatic and spontaneous, though, because one does not make any effort to experience more refined thought — the process continues by itself.

8. Samadhi

Sama means *even*, or *steady*. *Dhi* is intellect. Maharishi thus defines *samadhi* as *stable intelligence*, the unbounded field of Transcendental Consciousness, the most fundamental value of intelligence. *Samadhi* does not refer to the intellect, he explains, because intellect is a localized value of intelligence, whereas intelligence specifies a universal structure. *Samadhi* is a state of Yoga, but experiencing it also cultivates Yoga in higher states of consciousness.[34]

These eight limbs together constitute the body of Yoga. They are not, as often thought, a description of the path to Yoga, but taken together they provide a comprehensive vision of the structure of Yoga on every level. This is the Yoga Sutra's description of life in integration, in Unity. It reveals the glorious connection between individuality and universality, between individual life and cosmic life.

12
Karma Yoga, Gyan Yoga, Bhakti Yoga, and Raja Yoga

There are many types of Yoga instruction available today, designed for the varying needs and desires of an ever-expanding population of enthusiasts. For those seeking physical fitness, there are *Hatha Yoga* postures and exercises. Those interested in spiritual growth and fulfillment can take advantage of meditation, philosophy, purification techniques, and so forth. Regardless of one's requirements, there are books, web sites, or advertisements dedicated to fulfilling the need.

Aside from a few practices created by some modern instructors, most are related to one of the four main traditional categories of Yoga — *Karma Yoga*, *Gyan Yoga*, *Bhakti Yoga*, and *Raja Yoga*. Scholars and practitioners tend to view these as different methods with distinct procedures and philosophies.

Maharishi has discussed each in his writings and lectures, commenting on their ancient application as well as their modern interpretations. This chapter will examine Maharishi's comments on these four paths and how they relate to his Transcendental Meditation program.

Karma Yoga

Karma Yoga is thought to be the path of selfless action and service to others. According to many modern commentators, a life of service will purify the aspirant, and provide the foundation for a spiritual life. Indeed commentators on the Bhagavad-Gita often consider the term *Yoga* to be a reference to such a lifestyle. These interpretations are usually based on key verses that appear to support this view, such as the following:

तस्मादसक्तः सततं कार्यं कर्म समाचर
असक्तो ह्याचरन्कर्म परमाप्नोति पूरुषः

*Tasmād asaktaḥ satataṃ kāryaṃ karma samāchara
asakto hyācharan karma paramāpnoti pūrushaḥ*
(Bhagavad-Gita 3.19)

Therefore, remaining unattached, always do action worthy of performance. Engaging in action truly unattached, man attains to the Supreme.

Modern interpretations of Karma Yoga appear reasonable here, for at first glance Lord Krishna seems to advocate an attitude of non-attachment to actions and their results. According to this analysis, such behavior will ultimately lead the aspirant to "the Supreme," to higher states of consciousness.

Maharishi strongly disagrees. He holds that this verse does not suggest an attitude or philosophy, but is instead describing the reality of life in Cosmic Consciousness. In this state one experiences the Self as separate from activity — a natural state of non-attachment and perfect freedom. By living this state of separation one ultimately rises to God Consciousness and eventually to Unity Consciousness — "the Supreme."

Maharishi emphasizes that activity alone will never bring higher states of consciousness. Realizing these exalted levels of life requires the direct experience of Transcendental Consciousness, and this comes only from going deep within.

There is, however, a great value to activity. As Maharishi explains, it is neither activity alone that brings us to higher states of consciousness nor is it just meditation. One must meditate *and* act — one must dive deep within and then engage in one's normal activities. The purpose of activity is that it stabilizes the nervous system in the experience of pure consciousness — it allows the nervous system to become increasingly accustomed to maintaining the silence of Yoga along with the active phases of life. Maharishi explains:

> In order that transcendental bliss-consciousness may be lived at all times, it is necessary that it should not be lost when the mind comes out of meditation and engages in activity. For this to be possible the mind has to become so intimately familiar with the state of Being that it remains grounded in the mind at all times, through all the mental activity of thinking, discriminating and deciding, and through all phases of action on the sensory level. For this in turn, it is necessary that the process of gaining transcendental consciousness through meditation and that of engaging in activity should be alternated, so that transcendental consciousness and the waking

state of consciousness may come close together and finally merge into one another to give rise to the state of cosmic consciousness, the state in which one lives bliss consciousness, the inner awareness of Being, through all the activity of the waking and dreaming states and through the silence of the deep sleep state.[1]

For most of us, the ideal is to continue with our customary routines. Whether we are a doctor, construction worker, student, artist, or parent, we would simply continue with our normal lives, supplemented with Transcendental Meditation practice. But maintaining an attitude of non-attachment or surrender is not useful, and in Maharishi's view has no place in the proper understanding of Karma Yoga.[2] Karma Yoga is not a philosophy of life based on action, as modern interpreters and teachers suggest, but rather a practice whose basis is the regular experience of Yoga supplemented with activity.

Gyan Yoga

Gyan* Yoga is said to be the Yoga of contemplation. In some interpretations, Gyan Yoga encourages us to examine the truth of who and what we are, which is said to lead us to enlightenment.

Maharishi, on the other hand, feels that the principal component of Gyan Yoga is Yoga — the practice of going within and experiencing the Self. The difference between

---

* *Gyan* can also be spelled *jnana*. Maharishi preferred *gyan* for those not conversant with Sanskrit rules of pronunciation.

Karma Yoga and Gyan Yoga, then, is not the practice of Yoga meditation — that is common to both — but rather the nature of the practitioner's daily activity. A *Karma Yogi* practices the Transcendental Meditation technique and stabilizes its effects through action, whereas a *Gyani* also transcends but engages in knowledge and the activity of intellectual discernment. Yoga is common to both paths, but the daily activity depends upon the Yogi's lifestyle.

An obvious question, then, is "Which is better?" Or perhaps, "Which is better for me?" Maharishi's response is that Karma Yoga is the path for the person of action, but for the recluse — who lives away from society — the Yoga of Contemplation, Gyan Yoga, is more appropriate. As he explains:

> Both paths are equally valid for developing cosmic consciousness. Karma Yoga and Gyan Yoga each presents a direct way to fulfillment, but the path chosen should suit the way of life and the natural tendencies of the aspirant. A householder should not try to realize through Sankhya or Gyan Yoga: let him adopt the path of Karma Yoga and, fulfilling the aspirations of a life in the world, he will gain cosmic consciousness in a natural and harmonious manner. Similarly, a recluse, or sanyasi, should not aspire to adopt the path of Karma Yoga. He should follow the Sankhya teaching, or Gyan Yoga, and fulfilling the aspirations of a recluse way of life, he also will attain cosmic consciousness in a natural and harmonious manner.[3]

In the *Sankhya* teaching, to which Maharishi refers, one pursues intellectual understanding of the nature of reality. In this context it is equivalent to *Gyan Yoga* — the path of the recluse.

Bhakti Yoga

Bhakti Yoga, often referred to simply as *Bhakti*, is the path of devotion. In the modern world it is mostly understood as devotion to the divine — either God, a personal form of God, or the enlightened Guru (teacher). It can take many forms and include such devotional activities as singing, dancing, and prayer. It is often referred to as the path of love and service, and according to its proponents the act of devotion will bring one to higher levels of consciousness.

In Maharishi's teaching, however, devotion is a spontaneous product of the growth of higher states of consciousness, and not a practice, mood, or attitude. In Cosmic Consciousness the heart is filled with eternal bliss and love, which flows outward into the environment. One feels infinite love "at the sight of everything, at the hearing of everything, at the smelling of everything, at the tasting of anything, at the touch of anything."[4] In this way, the "ocean of Being" rises in waves of devotion, refining the physiology and stimulating the senses to perceive increasingly subtle levels of the surrounding environment. As a result of this spontaneous devotion, Cosmic Consciousness grows into God Consciousness, which is defined in part by the ability to perceive the most refined, celestial level of the material environment. And from God Consciousness, Unity Consciousness ultimately emerges.[5]

Bhakti, or devotion, is the subject of many passages from the Vedic literature, including sections of the Bhagavad-Gita and Shrimad Bhagavatam. These texts state that it is through devotion that one attains the highest level of consciousness, which has unfortunately led to the mistaken notion that one need not experience the inner Self — that one must only attend to devotional practices.

Maharishi emphasizes, however, that devotion in its most profound sense is an experiential reality that arises as a spontaneous result of the growth of consciousness. It is this infinite devotion that brings one to God Consciousness and ultimately to Unity Consciousness, not the idea of devotion or devotional practices.

It is also the case that devotional practices are natural for some people. These are also part of Bhakti, but Maharishi emphasizes again that Yoga — the direct experience of the eternal bliss and freedom within — is the basis of their success. And without transcending it is not possible to experience the most profound value of Bhakti:

> It is this transcendental state of Being which enables a man to become a Karma Yogi, one who is successful on the path of action. It is this that enables a man to become a bhakta, one who is successful on the path of devotion, and it is this that enables a man to become a gyani, one who is successful on the path of knowledge. This is the highway to the fulfillment of life's purpose.[6]

Maharishi further points out that to find God we must first find ourself — we must unfold our own consciousness as a prerequisite to any devotional practice:

> If a man wants to be a true devotee of God, he has to become his pure Self; he has to free himself from those attributes

which do not belong to him, and then only can he have one-pointed devotion. If he is enveloped by what he is not, then his devotion will be covered by that foreign element. His devotion will not reach God, and the love and blessings of God will not reach him. For his devotion to reach God, it is necessary that he should first become purely himself, covered by nothing. Then the process of devotion will connect him directly with the Lord, thereby bestowing on him the status of a devotee.[7]

Raja Yoga

Raja Yoga means the *Yoga of Kings*, or the *Royal Yoga*. Maharishi has said little of Raja Yoga other than an occasional comment that Transcendental Meditation practice is Raja Yoga in its most pure form, because there is nothing more royal than an effortless, natural path to the experience of Yoga. It is royal in that sense, but it is a technique for everyone, regardless of what they do in life.

Now we turn to a fascinating discovery by Tony Nader, MD, PhD, who found that the branches of the Vedic literature — including the texts of Yoga — correspond to different structures and functions of human physiology.

13
Yoga in Human Physiology

There is one more topic that is essential to our discussion of Yoga — the historic research of Dr. Tony Nader. Dr. Nader is a medical doctor with a PhD in brain and cognitive science, who discovered that the forty branches of Veda and the Vedic literature correspond to the forty main divisions of human physiology. In the context of Yoga, he found that the Patanjali Yoga Sutras are mirrored in the structure and function of the human brain.

To understand the significance of this research we need to first consider the nature of Veda and its literature. In recent history the term Veda has referred to four branches of Sanskrit literature (Rk Veda, Sama Veda, Yajur Veda, and Atharva Veda) along with some ancillary texts. Maharishi, however, offers a more profound understanding that locates Veda far beyond the realm of books on a shelf. In the following sections we will discuss Maharishi's analysis and how it relates to human physiology, and on that basis examine some of the main principles from Dr. Nader's research, especially as it pertains to Yoga.

Veda — the dynamic structure of pure consciousness
Pure consciousness, we have seen, is the most basic level of subjectivity, the source of our thoughts, intellect, feelings, and

creativity. But it is vastly more than this. It is also the silent ocean of Being underlying creation — a field of pure wakefulness, infinite and eternal, in which all the activities of life are created and administered. Though a silent and unchanging state of pure existence, it is nonetheless the source of all that there is — stars and galaxies, continents and mountain ranges, molecules and subatomic particles, and of course our own physiology.

So how does this abstract ocean of intelligence express itself as the material universe? In Maharishi's account, the impulse to create begins with a "stir" within the silent ocean of consciousness, as pure consciousness begins to move within itself. Being fully awake, it knows itself, it interacts with itself, and this self-interaction creates a flow within its silent structure.[1] Even though pure consciousness is eternally silent, its nature is to flow, but it does so without ever disrupting its eternal silence.

Madhuchhandas, the first Rishi, or Seer, of Rk Veda, saw this silence in motion within his own consciousness, which Maharishi describes as follows:

> There is a flow. So what is flowing? He didn't know in the beginning. He could only say 'flowing.' There is a flow. And when he saw the flow, what is flowing? Only silence can flow. So he saw silence flowing.[2]

Thus Madhuchhandas saw two things: He saw a flow and he saw that it was silence that was flowing. This flow expresses itself in terms of sound, which Maharishi describes as a hum, or a kind of vibration.[3] It is not an audible sound that we hear through the ears, but an unmanifest, primordial "whisper" within the fabric of pure consciousness. If our nervous system is sufficiently refined — if it is without much stress — we can experience this sound as it reverberates within the silence of our inner Self.

Maharishi further explains that we might first hear a single, continuous hum. But as the nervous system becomes increasingly refined, we can perceive the individual sounds that make up the hum, and can explore them as the dynamics of our own consciousness. Maharishi describes our ability to hear these sounds within our own consciousness:

> On that level, those values of sound are there, and anyone can take one's awareness to that settled state where one is open to oneself. And one would hear those sounds, one would see those sounds.[4]

Maharishi notes that our capacity to hear the sounds is analogous to perceiving the noise of a crowd as we approach a busy marketplace. At first we simply hear the crowd noise as one homogeneous sound, but as we draw near we begin to hear the different voices, conversations, laughter, etc. In the same way, we might first hear just a single hum reverberating within our consciousness during meditation, but as the physiology becomes increasingly refined we can appreciate the multitude of individual sounds that make up the hum.

These sounds are, in Maharishi's words, the dynamics of the transformation of consciousness into matter, the mechanics through which abstract consciousness expresses itself as material forms and phenomena[5] — they are the most fundamental level of the laws of nature from which the entire universe emerges.[6] Thus, as Maharishi explains, this infinite ocean of silence is also infinitely dynamic. It is a field of infinite silence and infinite dynamism.[7] This may sound contradictory — infinite silence *and* infinite dynamism together — but it is the nature of pure consciousness, the reality of a field of intelligence that truly includes all possibilities within it.[8]

In Sanskrit these sounds are collectively known as Veda. Veda means *knowledge*, in this context referring to *total knowledge* — all that is, was, and will be, the complete knowledge of the unmanifest reality of life and all its expressions. The entire creation emerges from Veda, is sustained in Veda, and is administered by Veda, and therefore even on its primordial level Veda contains everything. It includes the structure of the material world, along with the principles underlying every discipline, every profession — every aspect of life. And since Veda is the dynamic structure of our own Self, each of us has the capacity to know anything and everything.[9]

The term Veda includes all the sounds, both the single holistic sound as well as its diverse components, but the individual sounds are also known as Vedic literature. Maharishi grouped the sounds into forty "clusters," which correspond to the forty principal qualities of intelligence within pure consciousness. Each of these forty qualities represents fundamental characteristics of natural law, and corresponds to one of the forty main divisions of Veda and the Vedic literature.*

Long ago, great Rishis — men and women with highly developed levels of consciousness — experienced the Vedic sounds as the fluctuations of their own consciousness and expressed them as a literature composed of syllables, words, verses, sutras, etc.[10] These expressions were passed down over the millennia through an oral tradition, and eventually transcribed into written texts. Today you can go to a library and see collections of Sanskrit texts, with titles such as Nyaya Sutra, Mahabharata, and Nirukta.

Maharishi emphasized time and again, though, that the Vedic literature on its most fundamental level is not the printed books in a library, but the sounds within the dynamic structure of pure consciousness — the pure expressions of nature's creative processes. And while the written records are often referred to as Vedic literature, it is more appropriate to say that the sounds themselves are the literature. When one experiences the state of Yoga deep within and hears the sounds and explores them, then one is truly studying Veda, much more so than when poring over pages of a book.

---

* For a more complete discussion of each of the forty branches of Veda and the Vedic literature, see Nader, T., *Human Physiology: Expression of Veda and the Vedic Literature*.

Veda in human physiology

If the universe is created by Veda, then logically we can infer that every expression contains the structure of Veda. In other words, the qualities, characteristics, and organization of Veda must be the essential constituents of everything throughout creation, including our physiology. In this sense Veda is like a blueprint of creation, for it contains in seed form all the diverse elements of our universe.

In 1994 Dr. Nader* tested this hypothesis under Maharishi's guidance. After comparing the organs and systems of human physiology with the branches of Vedic literature, he concluded that there is a perfect correspondence between the forty principal aspects of the human body and the forty branches of Vedic literature, in both structure and function.[11]

Structure and function of Veda and physiology

Physiological **structure** refers to anatomical makeup: The brain has four lobes, the heart has four chambers, etc. **Function** describes what that part of the physiology actually does: The musculoskeletal system provides support, stability, and our capacity to move around in a variety of ways; the brain not only helps us think and plan on the basis of conscious

---

* In 2001, Maharishi asked Dr. Nader to take on the administration of the Global Country of World Peace, the umbrella for all the universities, schools, and organizations comprising Maharishi's worldwide movement. At that time, Maharishi also gave him the title Maharaja Adhiraj Rajaraam.

mental activity, but also administers an immense number of autonomic functions.

The **structure** of the Vedic literature is its organization in books, chapters, sections, verses, sutras, etc. The **function** of a text of Vedic literature refers to the qualities of consciousness that it embodies as well as the areas of human life that it addresses. For example, Sthapatya Veda provides the principles of architecture and community planning, while Gandharva-Veda brings out the elements of Vedic music.

Yoga and the association fibers of the cerebral cortex
The Patanjali Yoga Sutra, which we have cited as a principal source of Yoga philosophy, is an aspect of the Vedic literature. This means that Patanjali did not compose the Yoga Sutra as one might write a book, but rather he *cognized* its sounds — he experienced the sounds within his own consciousness and recorded them as the sutras of Yoga.

Yoga, we recall, means *union*. On the level of pure consciousness, the sounds of Yoga are those that embody the unifying quality of pure consciousness — the quality of intelligence that keeps the diverse sounds unified in one holistic intelligence. In their more expressed value, the sutras describe the unified state of Yoga in terms of Transcendental Consciousness, Cosmic Consciousness, God Consciousness, and Unity Consciousness.

Dr. Nader found this unifying quality in the association fibers of the cerebral cortex. In his words:

> We live in a diversified universe. Our senses are constantly bombarded by millions of inputs and our physiology constantly performs millions of tasks to maintain its balance, integrity, and evolution. The conscious comprehension of this diversified complexity and the integration of differences occur through the unifying values of the association fibers of the cerebral cortex.[12]

These fibers are the axons of neurons located in the cortical gray matter, which unite different parts of the same cerebral hemisphere. There are two kinds of association fibers, those that connect adjacent gyri (short association fibers) and those that pass between more distant parts (long association fibers). The total number of association fibers can be divided into 195 sets, which correspond to the 195 sutras of the Yoga Sutra.[13] Dr. Nader further found a correspondence between the dimensions of the brain area and the length of the sutras: the longer sutras correspond to larger areas of the cortex, and the shorter sutras to smaller areas.[14]

Dr. Nader points out that the four *padas* (chapters) of the Yoga Sutra correspond to the four lobes of the cerebral cortex. The first, Samadhi Pada, corresponds to the occipital lobe; the Sadhana Pada corresponds to the frontal lobe; the Vibhuti Pada corresponds to the parietal lobe (including insula); and the Kaivalya Pada corresponds to the temporal lobe.[15]

Dr. Nader concludes his chapter on Yoga by reminding us that the sequence of sounds of the Yoga Sutra and the sequence of sounds underlying the formation of the association fibers is the same, for both are expressions of Veda. He recommends that we read the Yoga Sutra in Sanskrit with proper pronunciation or else listen to its recitation by Vedic Pandits. This will enliven the corresponding sounds in our physiology. Whether or not we understand the meaning is immaterial, for reading or hearing the sounds will cause them to resonate with the association fibers and the brain physiology to which the sutras correspond.[16]

Experiencing the sounds in this way will neutralize irregularities and imbalances and induce the brain to function more in the way it was designed. Any stress or impediments to proper functioning will be eliminated over time.[17] This will maintain the vitality and strength of the structure and function of the brain, leading to the integration of mind and body. And in Dr. Nader's words, "Integrated understanding, an integrated decision-making process, and integrated action means mistake-free action in accord with natural law."[18]

The suggestion to read or listen to the Yoga Sutra in Sanskrit can be generalized to all branches of the Vedic literature. Since each aspect of the literature is associated with specific anatomical structures and functions, reading or listening to any branch will enliven the intelligence underlying its corresponding physiological part. This will have a positive and powerful effect on the growth and evolution of consciousness.

Dr. Nader's research has profoundly important implications for our understanding of the relationship between consciousness and physiology. It demonstrates that the physiology is not only made of consciousness, but that its very structures and functions are a perfect reflection of Veda, the most fundamental level of nature's intelligence. As human beings, therefore, we not only have recourse to this intelligence through our deep meditations but also through our physiology — we can restore our body to proper functioning in accord with its original design, leading us to better health and more rapid growth to higher states of consciousness.

14

Yoga and the Fulfillment of Life: Dharma, Artha, Kama, Moksha

Throughout the Vedic literature there are references to four comprehensive goals (called *purusharthas*) that are thought to be the ultimate aim of life as well as the measures of our success. These are:

dharma — living in accord with natural law
artha — material comfort
kama — fulfillment of desires
moksha — enlightenment

Over time, these have become philosophical guidelines with which to guide and uphold behavior. It has generally been thought that we should pursue the fulfillment of each in order to assure our success — that we must try to live our life in accord with dharma, acquire material comfort, fulfill all desires, and attain enlightenment.

In Maharishi's view, however, these aren't ideals to be pursued with discipline and hard work. Rather, they are the automatic and spontaneous byproducts of the regular experience of our inner Self, the state of Yoga. Let's look at Maharishi's comments on each, so that we can better appreciate how Yoga fulfills life in the most natural and easy way.

Dharma

We explored dharma in some detail in Chapter 8. There we discovered its synonymity with the concept of natural law, the totality of all the laws of nature that administer the universe and guide all progress. Dharma is not a systematic codification of societal rules and conventions, it is the evolutionary force of nature guiding life toward greater prosperity, freedom, and ultimately higher states of consciousness. A principal goal, therefore, is life in accord with dharma, so that nature's own intelligence guides every aspect of our life and behavior.

Learning to live in accord with dharma is not an intellectual process. We needn't study lists of rules and regulations or read guidebooks on how to navigate our lives. It simply requires regular experience of pure consciousness, the home of all the laws of nature, so that natural law spontaneously supports our every thought and action.

Research on Transcendental Meditation practice lends support to this understanding. Not only does the brain begin to work more effectively and more coherently, but the entire physiology becomes stronger, more resilient to stress, and less prone to disease. Behavior also becomes more harmonious, appropriate, useful, and less damaging. All these changes come without instruction or advice from others — the only requirement is a few minutes of practice morning and evening. In this way, regular Transcendental Meditation practice fulfills the goal of dharma.

Artha

Artha literally means *wealth*, *property*, *money*, and in a more general sense *material comfort*. When we consider the purpose of accumulating objects, we can better appreciate the role of Yoga in fulfilling the pursuit of wealth.

The nature of life is to grow in happiness. The basic tendency of our life is always toward more fulfillment, more happiness, more success, or more influence. Accumulating wealth is simply a means to obtain happiness. But if happiness is complete, if fulfillment is total, then the goal of all material aspirations has been realized. Maharishi explains in his commentary on the Bhagavad-Gita:

> With the experience of eternal bliss, all such aspirations are completely satisfied, for to store more and more means of happiness is the only purpose of artha in all its aspects.[1]

This does not mean an enlightened person would need to give up wealth and comforts, but simply that the goal of artha would be fulfilled, and any continued pursuit would be a wave on the vast ocean of bliss.

Kama

Kama means *desire*. Chapter 10 considered the role and importance of desire as well as the mistaken notion that we must forcibly relinquish it. Desire is not intrinsically an obstacle to the evolution of consciousness — in fact it is one of our greatest allies. But the continued desire for material happiness can keep us bound to the world. The solution is not to obstruct desire, but rather to experience the perfect happiness inherent within Yoga, which fulfills all goals and aspirations, thus fulfilling the role of desire.

> Desire naturally aims at happiness and the removal of suffering. All aspirations on this level are satisfied when man realizes the eternal bliss of the Self. When one seeks no more and desires no greater happiness, then one is fulfilled from the point of view of kama.²

Moksha

Moksha literally means *liberation*. In its most profound and most common usage it refers to enlightenment — liberation from ignorance and the realization of our true nature. Our ultimate goal is life in higher states of consciousness, and that is fulfilled through the regular experience of Yoga during Transcendental Meditation practice and the enjoyment of Yoga in higher states of consciousness.

Fulfillment

The nature of life is to grow toward more and more happiness, greater and greater fulfillment. We have encountered this theme throughout the preceding chapters, and we have seen how repeated experience of Yoga can satisfy it. When a natural method of experiencing Yoga was lost to view in recent centuries, the philosophies of strain and suffering became a seemingly inseparable part of the pursuit of higher states of consciousness. But now in this scientific age we find the knowledge of Yoga restored, so that any individual and any society can rise above problems and suffering, and enjoy a happy and productive life. For this we need only look within, and experience the infinite bliss inherent within our own nature.

Summary and Conclusion

In the preceding chapters, we have seen that Yoga is far more than simply a collection of physical exercises, however valuable these might be. It is, on one hand, the inner Self, an infinite reservoir of creativity and intelligence lying deep within each of us, the source of all our thoughts, dreams, hopes, and aspirations. And it is also the so-called "path of Yoga" —those techniques and procedures that allow us to dive deep inside and experience our hidden potential. The Transcendental Meditation technique, which Maharishi brought to light from the Vedic tradition, exemplifies this sense of Yoga, for it allows anyone to enjoy the silent depths of their inner Self and bring its qualities out into their active life, for more progress, happiness, and success.

Maharishi's meditation is so natural and effortless that anyone with the ability to think a thought can practice it effectively. But its ease and simplicity is more than a convenience — it is the reason it works. Meditations that involve concentration, such as staring at a candle or emptying the mind of thoughts, will not allow us to go inward, for the increased mental activity only serves to distance us from the silence of the state of Yoga. Likewise, techniques involving contemplation, such as considering and analyzing ideas or philosophies, will also keep the mind bound to its surface,

SUMMARY AND CONCLUSION

and prevent the awareness from settling within. The inner state of Yoga is infinitely silent, with no thoughts or mental excitations, and in order to experience it the mind must follow a natural course toward its progressively quiet levels. The Transcendental Meditation program is easy to practice and easy to learn under the guidance of a qualified instructor.

The purpose of Yoga practice, though, is not merely to enjoy pure consciousness during the silence of daily meditation. We practice the Transcendental Meditation technique to get more out of life — to be more productive, successful, healthy, and happy. According to the ancient Yoga texts, we have infinite potential; there are no limits to our creativity, intelligence, or bliss, and scientific research has repeatedly demonstrated that growth in this direction is available through Transcendental Meditation practice.

The immediate benefits of experiencing the state of Yoga are compelling. Improved health, more access to our mental potential, and better relationships are important to us all. In the beginning days of practice, we may be delighted with less stress, lower blood pressure, clearer thinking, or more happiness, but these are just the beginning. The benefits are cumulative, and the longer we meditate the more rich and profound they become. Maharishi's discussion of higher states of consciousness provides a vision of the goal through which we can gauge our progress and enjoy our growth in fulfillment, peace, and self-sufficiency.

Regaining the lost knowledge of Yoga

Yoga practice is ancient, but over the centuries the purity of its tradition has become obscured and misunderstood. When the effortless technique for experiencing Yoga became unavailable, sincere teachers mistook the goal for the path, and created philosophies and techniques based upon descriptions of higher states of consciousness. For example, when reading of the fulfillment and self-sufficiency of the enlightened state, some have thought that we should rid ourselves of desires, remain unattached to the material world, and maintain an attitude of equanimity. But as Maharishi points out, these practices do not allow the awareness to experience the infinite intelligence and creativity of the state of Yoga. Furthermore, the qualities of higher states of consciousness, such as fulfillment and self-sufficiency, unfold spontaneously from regular Transcendental Meditation practice, not from adopting an attitude, mood, or philosophy.

How could such precious knowledge become distorted and lost? Maharishi speaks of it as part of a larger cycle of life, noting that it is natural to lose something that is unseen:

> If the occupants of a house forget the foundations, it is because the foundations lie underground, hidden from view. It is no surprise that Being was lost to view, for It lies in the transcendental field of life.[1]

With this loss of proper understanding of Yoga, many key areas of its philosophy became distorted. Karma Yoga was thought to be a life of service, Gyan Yoga became contemplation without Yoga, and the role of Yoga in Bhakti was obscured. Maharishi's point, however, is that Yoga is the foundation of every practice and every lifestyle, and that these beautiful areas of life can once again become rich and fulfilling, and flourish in the effortless growth to higher states of consciousness.

Our brain corresponds to the Yoga Sutra

The research of Tony Nader, MD, PhD, which we discussed in Chapter 14, is truly one of the most extraordinary elements of Yoga philosophy. Dr. Nader discovered that the structure and function of the Yoga Sutra corresponds to the structure and function of the human brain. This remarkable research demonstrates that the human physiology is made of consciousness, and that we can grow toward higher states of consciousness not only from our twice-daily practice of the Transcendental Meditation program, but also from reading the Vedic literature with proper pronunciation, and listening to the recitations of Vedic Pandits.

Maharishi has revitalized the ancient philosophy of Yoga. He has rescued it from the mire of mysticism and restored it to its proper place in human life — as an effortless, natural science and technology of human evolution, at once ancient and yet thoroughly modern. With this great revival of knowledge, every individual has the master key to restore the true dignity of human life.

Additional Readings

Books

Maharishi Mahesh Yogi. *Maharishi Mahesh Yogi on the Bhagavad-Gita: A New Translation and Commentary, Chapters 1–6.* London: Arkana, 1990.

Maharishi Mahesh Yogi. *Science of Being and Art of Living.* New York: Plume publications, 2001.

Maharishi Mahesh Yogi. *Maharishi's Absolute Theory of Government: Automation in Administration.* Vlodrop, The Netherlands: Age of Enlightenment Publications, 1994.

Nader, Tony. *Human Physiology: Expression of Veda and the Vedic Literature.* Vlodrop, The Netherlands: Maharishi Vedic University Press, 1994.

Nader, Tony. *Ramayan in Human Physiology.* Fairfield, IA: Maharishi University of Management Press, 2012.

Sands, William F. *Maharishi Mahesh Yogi and His Gift to the World.* Fairfield, IA: MUM Press, 2012.

Wallace, Robert Keith. *The Physiology of Consciousness.* Fairfield, IA: MUM Press, 1993.

Internet

www.tm.org (Transcendental Meditation program, US)

www.mum.edu (Maharishi University of Management)

www.davidlynchfoundation.org (David Lynch Foundation)

www.istpp.org (Institute of Science, Technology and Public Policy at Maharishi University of Management)

References

Introduction

1. William James, *The Varieties of Religious Experience* (New York: Mentor-Nal, 1958), 296.

Chapter 1

1. All translations from the Bhagavad-Gita are Maharishi's.

2. Maharishi Mahesh Yogi, *Maharishi Mahesh Yogi on the Bhagavad-Gita: A New Translation and Commentary, Chapters 1–6* (Arkana, 1990), 126. [Original work printed in 1967.]

3. Ibid., 129.

4. Maharishi Mahesh Yogi, *Science of Being and Art of Living* (New York, NY: Plume publications, 2001), 8. [Original work printed in 1963.]

5. Maharishi Mahesh Yogi, *Life Supported by Natural Law* (Washington, DC: Age of Enlightenment Press, 1986), 25.

6. Maharishi, *Science of Being and Art of Living*, 6.

7. Ibid., 29.

8. *Maharishi Mahesh Yogi on the Bhagavad-Gita*, 135.

9. Nṛisiṁhottaratāpanīya Upanishad, *1*, trans. Maharishi Mahesh Yogi.

Chapter 2

1. Maharishi, *Science of Being and Art of Living*, 4.

2. *Creating an Ideal Society* (Rheinweiler, W. Germany: Maharishi European University Press, 1976), 123.

3. Maharishi, *Science of Being and Art of Living*, 30.

4. "Are All Meditation Techniques the Same?" Online at: Maharishi University of Management; about MUM, research; research institute center; center for brain, consciousness, and cognition; categories of meditation.

Chapter 3

1. Katha Upanishad, 1.3.12, trans. W.F. Sands.
2. Katha Upanishad, 2.3.17, trans. W.F. Sands.
3. Māṇdukya Upanishad, 3.37, trans. W.F. Sands.
4. Nṛisiṁhottaratāpanīya Upanishad 1, trans. Maharishi.
5. First four experiences are from *Invincible America Assembly: Experiences of Higher States of Consciousness of Course Participants, Volume 1, 2006–2009* (Fairfield, IA: MUM Press, 2012).
6. *Creating an Ideal Society*, 82.
7. Ibid., 77.
8. P. Gallois, "Modifications Neurophysiologiques et Respiratoires lors de la Pratique des Techniques de Relaxation," *L'Encéphale* 10 (1984): 139–44.
9. J. O'Halloran, R. Jevning, A.F. Wilson, R. Skowsky, R.N. Walsh, and C.N. Alexander, "Hormonal Control in a State of Decreased Activation: Potentiation of Arginine Vasopressin Secretion," *Physiology and Behavior* 35(4) (1985): 591–95.
10. R. Jevning, A.F. Wilson, W.R. Smith, and M.E. Morton, "Redistribution of Blood Flow in Acute Hypometabolic Behavior," *American Journal of Physiology* 235(1) (1978): R89–R92.
11. M.C. Dillbeck and D.W. Orme-Johnson, "Physiological Differences Between Transcendental Meditation and Rest," *American Psychologist* 42(9) (1987): 879–81.
12. J.P. Banquet and M. Sailhan, "EEG Analysis of Spontaneous and Induced States of Consciousness," *Revue d'Electroencéphalographie et de Neurophysiologie Clinique* 4 (1974): 445–53.
13. M.C. Dillbeck and E.C. Bronson, "Short-Term Longitudinal Effects of the Transcendental Meditation Technique on EEG Power and Coherence," *International Journal of Neuroscience* 14(3/4) (1981): 147–51.
14. M.C. Dillbeck et al., "Frontal EEG Coherence, H-Reflex Recovery, Concept Learning, and the TM-Sidhi Program," *In-*

ternational Journal of Neuroscience 15(3) (1981): 151–57; M.C. Dillbeck and E.C. Bronson, "Short-Term Longitudinal Effects of the Transcendental Meditation Technique on EEG Power and Coherence," *International Journal of Neuroscience* 147–51; D.W. Orme-Johnson and J.T. Farrow, eds., *Scientific Research on the Transcendental Meditation Program: Collected Papers, Vol. 1* (Rheinweiler, W. Germany: MERU Press, 1977), 208–12.

15. C. Gaylord, D.W. Orme-Johnson, and F. Travis, "The Effects of the Transcendental Meditation Technique and Progressive Muscular Relaxation on EEG Coherence, Stress Reactivity, and Mental Health in Black Adults," *International Journal of Neuroscience* 46(1/2) (1989): 77–86.

16. K. Badawi, R.K. Wallace, D.W. Orme-Johnson, and A.M. Rouzeré, "Electrophysiologic Characteristics of Respiratory Suspension Periods Occurring During the Practice of the Transcendental Meditation Program," *Psychosomatic Medicine* 46(3) (1984): 267–76.

17. S.M. Brown, "Unity and Diversity in Maharishi Vedic Science, Higher States of Consciousness, and a Study of Undergraduate Student Development," (Doctoral Dissertation), available from ProQuest Dissertation and Theses database. (UMI No. 9427917.)

18. Ibid.

Chapter 4

1. R.W. Cranson, D.W. Orme-Johnson, M.C. Dillbeck, C.H. Jones, C.N. Alexander, and J. Gackenbach, "Transcendental Meditation and Improved Performance on Intelligence-Related Measures: A Longitudinal Study," *Journal of Personality and Individual Differences* 12 (1991): 1105–16.

2. K.T. So and D.W. Orme-Johnson, "Three Randomized Experiments on the Holistic Longitudinal Effects of the Transcendental Meditation Technique on Cognition," *Intelligence* 2001 29(5): 419–440.

3. D.E. Miskiman, "The Effect of the Transcendental Medi-

tation program on the organization of thinking and recall (secondary organization," In D.W. Orme-Johnson and J.T. Farrow, eds., *Scientific Research on the Transcendental Meditation Program: Collected Papers, Vol. 1* (Rheinweiler, W. Germany: MERU Press, 1977), 385–92.

4. M. De Fatima Campos Belham, "Introduction in a Military Academy the Transcendental Meditation Program for Prevention of Stress," in M. Dillbeck, ed., *Scientific Research on Maharishi's Transcendental Meditation and TM-Sidhi Program: Collected Papers, Vol. 6,* (printed in China for Maharishi Vedic University, Vlodrop, The Netherlands, 2011), 4068–72.

5. S.I. Nidich, R.J. Nidich, and M. Rainforth, "School Effectiveness: Achievement Gains at Maharishi School of the Age of Enlightenment," *Education* 107 (1986): 49–54.

6. D.W. Orme-Johnson and C.T. Haynes, "EEG Phase Coherence, Pure Consciousness, Creativity, and TM-Sidhi Experiences," *International Journal of Neuroscience* 13(4) (1981): 211–217; M.C. Dillbeck et al., "Frontal EEG Coherence, H-Reflex Recovery, Concept Learning, and the TM-Sidhi Program," *International Journal of Neuroscience* 15(3) (1981).

7. D.P. Heaton and D.W. Orme-Johnson, "The Transcendental Meditation Program and Academic Achievement," in D.W. Orme-Johnson and J.T. Farrow, eds., *Scientific Research on the Transcendental Meditation Program: Collected Papers, Vol. 1* (Rheinweiler, W. Germany: MERU Press, 1977), 396-99.

8. P. Kember, "The Transcendental Meditation Technique and Postgraduate Academic Performance," *British Journal of Educational Psychology* 55 (1985): 164–66.

Chapter 5

1. M.H. Teicher, J.A. Samson, Y.S. Sheu, A. Polcari, and C.E. McGreenery, "Hurtful Words: Association of Exposure to Peer Verbal Abuse With Elevated Psychiatric Symptom Scores and Corpus Callosum Abnormalities," *American Journal of Psychiatry* 167 (2010): 1464–71.

REFERENCES

2. R.M. Thomas, G. Hotsenpiller, and D. Peterson, "Acute Psychosocial Stress Reduces Cell Survival in Adult Hippocampal Neurogenesis without Altering Proliferation," *Journal of Neuroscience*, 27(11) (2007): 2734-43.

3. K. Eppley, A. Abrams, and J. Shear, "Differential Effects of Relaxation Techniques on Trait Anxiety: A Meta-Analysis," *Journal of Clinical Psychology* 45(6) (1989): 957–74.

4. C.N. Alexander, G.C. Swanson, M. Rainforth, T.W. Carlisle, C.C. Todd, and R.M. Oates, "Effects of the Transcendental Meditation Program on Stress Reduction, Health, and Employee Development: A Prospective Study in Two Occupational Settings," *Anxiety, Stress, and Coping* 6 (1993): 245–62.

5. T. Haratani and T. Hemmi, "Effects of Transcendental Meditation on Mental Health of Industrial Workers," *Japanese Journal of Industrial Health* 32 (1990): 656.

6. J. Childs, "The Use of the Transcendental Meditation Program as a Therapy with Juvenile Offenders," *Dissertation Abstracts International*, 34 (8-A, Pt. 1) (1974): 4732–33.

7. A.I. Abrams and L.M. Siegel, "The Transcendental Meditation Program and Rehabilitation at Folsom State Prison: A Cross-Validation Study," *Criminal Justice and Behavior* 5(1) (1978): 3–20.

8. S.J. Grosswald, W.R. Stixrud, F. Travis, and M.A. Bateh, "Use of the Transcendental Meditation Technique to Reduce Symptoms of Attention Deficit Hyperactivity Disorder (ADHD) by Reducing Stress and Anxiety: An Exploratory Study," online at: *Current Issues in Education*, 10(2), (http://cie.ed.asu.edu/volume10/number2/).

9. "World Health Organization. Cardiovascular Disease. Fact sheet N°317, Geneva, September 2009," online at: World Health Organization); media centre; fact sheets; cardiovascular disease.

10. "Heart Disease and Stroke Statistics—2011 Update: A Report From the American Heart Association," online at: *Circulation*, February, 2011 (http://circ.ahajournals.org).

11. M. Rainforth, R.H. Schneider, S.I. Nidich, C. Gaylord-King, J.W. Salerno, J.W. Anderson, "Stress Reduction Programs in Patients with Elevated Blood Pressure: A Systematic Review and Meta-Analysis," *Current Hypertension Reports* 9(6) (2007): 520–28.

12. J.W. Anderson, C. Liu, and R.J. Kryscio, "Blood Pressure Response to Transcendental Meditation: A Meta-Analysis," *American Journal of Hypertension* 21(3) (2008): 310–16.

13. M. Paul-Labrador, et al., "Effects of a Randomized Controlled Trial of Transcendental Meditation on Components of the Metabolic Syndrome in Subjects with Coronary Heart Disease," *Archives of Internal Medicine* 166(11) (2006): 1218–24.

14. R. Jayadevappa, J.C. Johnson, B.S. Bloom, S. Nidich, S. Desai, S. Chhatre, et al., "Effectiveness of Transcendental Meditation on Functional Capacity and Quality of Life of African Americans with Congestive Heart Failure: A Randomized Control Study," *Ethnicity and Disease* 17 (2007): 72–77.

15. V.A. Barnes, F.A. Treiber, and M.H. Johnson, "Impact of Stress Reduction on Ambulatory Blood Pressure in African American Adolescents." *American Journal of Hypertension* 17(4) (2004): 366–69.

16. J.Z. Fields, K.W. Walton, R.H. Schneider, S.I. Nidich, R. Pomerantz, P Suchdev, et al., "Effect of a Multimodality Natural Medicine Program on Carotid Atherosclerosis in Older Subjects: A Pilot Trial of Maharishi Vedic Medicine," *American Journal of Cardiology* 89(8) (2002): 952–58.

17. M. Paul-Labrador, et al., "Effects of a Randomized Controlled Trial of Transcendental Meditation on Components of the Metabolic Syndrome in Subjects with Coronary Heart Disease," *Archives of Internal Medicine* 166(11) (2006): 1218–24.

18. A. Castillo-Richmond, R.H. Schneider, C.N. Alexander, R. Cook, H. Myers, S. Nidich, et al., "Effects of Stress Reduction on Carotid Atherosclerosis in Hypertensive African Americans," *Stroke* 31(3) (2000): 568–73.

19. R.H. Schneider, C.N. Alexander, F. Staggers, D.W. Orme-Johnson, M. Rainforth, J. Salerno, et al., "A Randomized Controlled Trial of Stress Reduction in African Americans Treated for Hypertension for over One Year," *American Journal of Hypertension* 18(1) (2005): 88–98.

20. M. Paul-Labrador, et al., "Effects of a Randomized Controlled Trial of Transcendental Meditation on Components of the Metabolic Syndrome in Subjects with Coronary Heart Disease," *Archives of Internal Medicine* 166(11) (2006): 1218–24.

21. V.A. Barnes, F.A. Treiber, J.R. Turner, H. Davis, W.B. Strong, "Acute Effects of Transcendental Meditation on Hemodynamic Functioning in Middle-Aged Adults," *Psychosomatic Medicine* 61(4) (1999): 525–31.

22. R.H. Schneider, C.N. Alexander, F. Staggers, M. Rainforth, J.W. Salerno, A. Hartz, et al., "Long-Term Effects of Stress Reduction on Mortality in Persons >/=55 Years of Age with Systemic Hypertension," *American Journal of Cardiology* 95(9) (2005): 1060–64.

23. M. Cooper and M. Aygen, "Transcendental Meditation in the Management of Hypercholesterolemia," *Journal of Human Stress* 5(4) (1979): 24–27.

24. L.C. Fergusson, A.J. Bonsheck, G. Le Masson, "Vedic Science Based Education and Mental and Physical Health: A Preliminary Longitudinal Study in Cambodia," *Journal of Instructional Psychology* 22 (1995): 308–319.

25. C.N. Alexander, et al., "Effects of the Transcendental Meditation Program on Stress Reduction, Health, and Employee Development," *Anxiety, Stress, and Coping* 6 (1993).

26. T. Haratani and T. Hemmi, "Effects of Transcendental Meditation on Mental Health of Industrial Workers," *Japanese Journal of Industrial Health* 32 (1990).

27. R.E. Herron and S.L. Hillis, "The Impact of the Transcendental Meditation Program on Government Payments to Physicians in Quebec: An Update—Accumulative Decline of 55%

Over a 6-Year Period," *American Journal of Health Promotion* 14(5) (2000): 284–91.

28. D.W. Orme-Johnson, "Medical Care Utilization and the Transcendental Meditation Program," *Psychosomatic Medicine* 49(1) (1987): 493–507.

29. D.W. Orme-Johnson and R.E. Herron, "An Innovative Approach to Reducing Medical Care Utilization and Expenditures," *American Journal of Managed Care* 3(1) (1997): 135–144.

30. R.K. Wallace, M.C. Dillbeck, E. Jacobe, and B. Harrington, "The Effects of the Transcendental Meditation and TM-Sidhi Program on the Aging Process," *International Journal of Neuroscience* 16(1) (1982): 53–58.

31. J.L. Glaser, J.L. Brind, J.H. Vogelman, M.J. Eisner, M.C. Dillbeck, R.K. Wallace, et al., "Elevated Serum Dehydroepiandrosterone Sulfate Levels in Practitioners of the Transcendental Meditation (TM) and TM-Sidhi Programs," *Journal of Behavioral Medicine* 15(4) (1992): 327–41.

32. C.N. Alexander, V.A. Barnes, R.H. Schneider, E.J. Langer, R.I. Newman, H.M. Chandler, J.L. Davies, and M. Rainforth, "A Randomized Controlled Trial of Stress Reduction on Cardiovascular and All-Cause Mortality in the Elderly: Results of 8 and 15 year Follow-Ups," *Circulation* 93 (1996): 629. Abstract.

33. R.H. Schneider, C.N. Alexander, F. Staggers, M. Rainforth, J.W. Salerno, A. Hartz, et al., "Long-Term Effects of Stress Reduction on Mortality in Persons >/=55 Years of Age with Systemic Hypertension," *American Journal of Cardiology* 95(9) (2005): 1060–64.

Chapter 6

1. W.F. Sands, "Natural Law in the Valmiki Ramayan in the Light of Maharishi's Vedic Science," *Modern Science and Vedic Science* 8, no. 1 (1998).

2. *Maharishi Mahesh Yogi on the Bhagavad-Gita*, 26.

3. Ibid., 30.

4. Ibid., 26–27.

5. Maharishi Mahesh Yogi, *Science, Consciousness and Ageing: Proceedings of the International Conference*, West Germany: Maharishi European Research University Press (1980): 75.

6. *Maharishi Mahesh Yogi on the Bhagavad-Gita*, 64.

7. S.I. Nidich, "A Study of the Relationship of the Transcendental Meditation program to Kohlberg's Stages of Moral Reasoning," *Dissertation Abstracts International* 36(7) (1976): 4361A.

8. M.C. Dillbeck, D.W. Orme-Johnson, and R.K. Wallace, "Frontal EEG Coherence, H-Reflex Recovery, Concept Learning, and the TM-Sidhi Program," *International Journal of Neuroscience* 15(3) (1981); D.W. Orme-Johnson and C.T. Haynes, "EEG Phase Coherence, Pure Consciousness, Creativity, and TM-Sidhi Experiences," *International Journal of Neuroscience*; D.W. Orme-Johnson and J.T. Farrow, eds., *Scientific Research on the Transcendental Meditation Program: Collected Papers, Vol. 1* (Rheinweiler, W. Germany: MERU Press, 1977), 208–12; R.A. Chalmers et al., eds., *Scientific Research on Maharishi's Transcendental Meditation and TM-Sidhi Program: Collected Papers, Vol. 4* (Vlodrop, The Netherlands: MVU Press, 1989), 2245–66.

9. S.I. Nidich, R.A. Ryncarz, A.I. Abrams, D.W. Orme-Johnson, and R.K. Wallace, "Kohlbergian Moral Perspective Responses, EEG Coherence, and the Transcendental Meditation and TM-Sidhi Program," *Journal of Moral Education* 12(3) (1983): 166–73.

10. V.A. Barnes, L.B. Bauza, and F.A. Treiber, "Impact of Stress Reduction on Negative School Behavior in Adolescents," *Health and Quality of Life Outcomes*, 1(1) (2003):10.

11. S.J. Grosswald, W.R. Stixrud, F. Travis, and M.A. Bateh, "Use of the Transcendental Meditation Technique to Reduce Symptoms of Attention Deficit Hyperactivity Disorder (ADHD)," *Current Issues in Education* [On-line] 2008 10(2).

12. J. Childs, "The Use of the Transcendental Meditation Program as a Therapy with Juvenile Offenders," *Dissertation Abstracts International*, 34 (8-A, Pt. 1) (1974).

13. C.R. Bleick and A.I. Abrams, "The Transcendental Meditation Program and Criminal Recidivism in California," *Journal of Criminal Justice* 15(3) (1987): 211–30.

14. A.I. Abrams and L.M. Siegel, "The Transcendental Meditation Program and Rehabilitation at Folsom State Prison: A Cross-Validation Study," *Criminal Justice and Behavior* 5(1) (1978).

15. C.N. Alexander and D.W. Orme-Johnson, "Walpole Study of the Transcendental Meditation Program in Maximum Security Prisoners II: Longitudinal Study of Development and Psychopathology," *Journal of Offender Rehabilitation* 36(1–4) (2003): 127–60.

16. "State of Recidivism: The Revolving Door of America's Prisons," online at: Pew Center on the States, (http://www.pewstates.org/uploadedFiles/PCS_Assets/2011/Pew_State_of_Recidivism.pdf).

17. Ibid.

18. C.N. Alexander and D.W. Orme-Johnson, "Walpole Study of the Transcendental Meditation Program in Maximum Security Prisoners II: Longitudinal Study of Development and Psychopathology," *Journal of Offender Rehabilitation* 36(1–4) (2003): 127–60.

19. J.S. Brooks and T. Scarano, "Transcendental Meditation in the Treatment of Post-Vietnam Adjustment," *Journal of Counseling and Development* 64 (1985): 212–15.

20. G.A. Ellis and P. Corum, "Removing the Motivator: A Holistic Solution to Substance Abuse," *Alcoholism Treatment Quarterly* 11(3/4) (1994): 271–96.

21. C.N. Alexander et al., "Effects of the Transcendental Meditation Program on Stress Reduction, Health, and Employee Development," *Anxiety, Stress, and Coping* 6 (1993).

22. T. Haratani and T. Hemmi, "Effects of Transcendental Meditation on Mental Health of Industrial Workers," *Japanese Journal of Industrial Health* 32 (1990).

23. G.A. Ellis and P. Corum, "Removing the Motivator: A Holistic Solution to Substance Abuse," *Alcoholism Treatment Quarterly* 11(3/4) (1994).

24. Ibid.

Chapter 7

1. *Maharishi Mahesh Yogi on the Bhagavad-Gita*, 428.

2. Ibid., 135.

3. Ibid.

4. Maharishi, *Science of Being and Art of Living*, 245.

5. *Maharishi Mahesh Yogi on the Bhagavad-Gita*, 314.

6. Maharishi, *Science of Being and Art of Living*, 245.

7. *Maharishi Mahesh Yogi on the Bhagavad-Gita*, 343.

8. Ibid., 135.

9. Maharishi, *Science of Being and Art of Living*, 247.

10. V. Katz, *Conversations with Maharishi: Maharishi Mahesh Yogi Speaks about the Full Development of Human Consciousness* (Fairfield, IA: MUM Press, 2011), 34.

11. Maharishi, *Science of Being and Art of Living*, 247.

12. Ibid., xviii.

13. Maharishi Vedic University, *Maharishi Vedic University: Exhibition*, (The Netherlands: Maharishi Vedic University Press, 1993), 148.

14. Ibid.

15. *Invincible America Assembly: Experiences of Higher States of Consciousness of Course Participants, Volume 1, 2006–2009* (Fairfield, IA: MUM Press, 2012).

16. Ibid.

17. The translations of the four Mahavakyas are Maharishi's.

18. *Maharishi Mahesh Yogi on the Bhagavad-Gita*, 357–58.

19. *Maharishi Vedic University: Exhibition* (The Netherlands: Maharishi Vedic University Press, 1993), 123.

20. *Maharishi Mahesh Yogi on the Bhagavad-Gita*, 449.

21. Ibid.

Chapter 8

1. Maharishi Mahesh Yogi, *Maharishi's Absolute Theory of Government: Automation in Administration* (Vlodrop, The Netherlands: Age of Enlightenment Publications, 1994), 308.

2. *Science, Consciousness, and Ageing*, 39.

3. Ibid.

4. Ibid.

5. Ibid.

6. Yogatattwa Upanishad 53–55, trans. W.F. Sands.

7. *Maharishi's Absolute Theory of Government: Automation in Administration*, 309.

8. *Life Supported by Natural Law*, 31.

9. *Invincible America Assembly: Experiences of Higher States of Consciousness of Course Participants, Volume 1, 2006–2009* (Fairfield, IA: MUM Press, 2012).

10. F. Travis and D.W. Orme-Johnson, "EEG Coherence and Power During Yogic Flying: Investigating the Mechanics of the TM-Sidhi Program," *International Journal of Neuroscience* 54(1/2) (1990): 1–12.

11. D.W. Orme-Johnson and C.T. Haynes, "EEG Phase Coherence, Pure Consciousness, Creativity, and TM-Sidhi Experiences," *International Journal of Neuroscience*; M.C. Dillbeck, D.W. Orme-Johnson, and R.K. Wallace, "Frontal EEG Coherence, H-Reflex Recovery, Concept Learning, and the TM-Sidhi

Program," *International Journal of Neuroscience* 15(3) (1981); D.W. Orme-Johnson and J.T. Farrow, eds., *Scientific Research on the Transcendental Meditation Program: Collected Papers, Vol. 1* (Rheinweiler, W. Germany: MERU Press, 1977), 208–12; R.A. Chalmers, et al., eds., *Scientific Research on Maharishi's Transcendental Meditation and TM-Sidhi Program, Collected Papers, Vol. 4* (Vlodrop, The Netherlands: MVU Press, 1989), 2245–66.

12. D.W. Orme-Johnson and P. Gelderloos, "Topographic Brain Mapping During Yogic Flying," *International Journal of Neuroscience* 38(3/4) (1988): 427–34.

13. A. Jedrczak, M. Beresford, and G. Clements, "The TM-Sidhi Program, Pure Consciousness, Creativity and Intelligence," *Journal of Creative Behavior* 19(4) (1985): 270–75.

14. M.C. Dillbeck et al., "Frontal EEG Coherence, H-Reflex Recovery, Concept Learning, and the TM-Sidhi Program," *International Journal of Neuroscience* 15(3) (1981).

15. P. Gelderloos, "Psychological Health and Development of Students at Maharishi International University: A Controlled Longitudinal Study," *Modern Science and Vedic Science* 1(4) (1987): 471–87.

16. Ibid.

Chapter 9

1. *His Holiness Maharishi Mahesh Yogi — Thirty Years Around the World: Dawn of the Age of Enlightenment, Volume I, 1957–1964* (The Netherlands: Maharishi Vedic University Press, 1986), 430.

2. *Maharishi Mahesh Yogi on the Bhagavad-Gita*, 318.

3. Ibid.

4. Yoga Sutra 2.35, trans. Maharishi Mahesh Yogi.

5. M.C. Dillbeck, G. Landrith III, and D.W. Orme-Johnson, "The Transcendental Meditation Program and Crime Rate Change in a Sample of Forty-Eight Cities," *Journal of Crime and Justice* 4 (1981): 25–45.

6. Maharishi Mahesh Yogi, *Enlightenment for Every Individual and Invincibility for Every Nation* (Rheinweiler, W. Germany: Maharishi European University Press, 1978), 87.

7. *Creating an Ideal Society*, 124.

8. Shiva Saṃhitā, 3.42, trans. W.F. Sands.

9. J.S. Hagelin et al., "Effects of Group Practice of the Transcendental Meditation Program on Preventing Violent Crime in Washington, DC: Results of the National Demonstration Project, June–July 1993," *Social Indicators Research* 47(2) (1999): 153–201.

10. "Transforming Political Institutions Through Individual and Collective Consciousness: The Maharishi Effect and Government," presented at the Annual Meeting of the American Political Science Association, Washington, DC, August 1997.

11. Paper presented at the Annual Meeting of the Midwest Political Science Association, Chicago, April 20, 2006.

12. W.F. Sands, *Maharishi Mahesh Yogi and His Gift to the World* (Fairfield, IA: MUM Press, 2012), 146–59.

13. R.A. Chalmers, G. Clements, H. Schenkluhn, and M. Weinless, eds., *Scientific Research on Maharishi's Transcendental Meditation and TM-Sidhi Program: Collected Papers, Vol. 4* (Vlodrop, The Netherlands: MVU Press, 1989), 2532–48.

14. M.C. Dillbeck et al., "Consciousness as a Field: The Transcendental Meditation and TM-Sidhi Program and Changes in Social Indicators," *The Journal of Mind and Behavior* 8 (1987): 67–104.

15. D.W. Orme-Johnson, C.N. Alexander, J.L. Davies, H.M. Chandler, and W.E. Larimore, "International Peace Project in the Middle East: The Effects of the Maharishi Technology of the Unified Field," *Journal of Conflict Resolution* 32(4) (1988): 776–812.

16. R.A. Chalmers, G. Clements, H. Schenkluhn, and M. Weinless, eds., *Scientific Research on Maharishi's Transcendental Meditation and TM-Sidhi Program: Collected Papers, Vol. 4* (Vlodrop, The Netherlands: MVU Press, 1989), 2730–62.

REFERENCES

17. D.W. Orme-Johnson, M.C. Dillbeck, and C.N. Alexander, "Preventing Terrorism and International Conflict: Effects of Large Assemblies of Participants in the Transcendental Meditation and TM-Sidhi Programs," *Journal of Offender Rehabilitation* 36(1–4) (2003): 283–302.

18. Maharishi Mahesh Yogi, *Maharishi's Absolute Theory of Defence: Sovereignty in Invincibility* (India: Age of Enlightenment Publications, 1996), 5.

Chapter 10

1. *Maharishi Mahesh Yogi on the Bhagavad-Gita*, preface.

2. Maharishi Mahesh Yogi, March 8, 2006, the Maharishi Channel, Video Archives, Press Conferences, press conferences 2006.

3. T.S. Rukmani (translator), *Yogavārttika of Vijñānabhikṣu*, (Delhi: Munshiram Manoharlal, 1981), 31.

4. Maharishi Mahesh Yogi. *Patanjali and the Eight Limbs of Yoga*. [videotaped lecture, 18 August, 1971, Humboldt State College, Arcata, CA, USA].

5. *Maharishi Mahesh Yogi on the Bhagavad-Gita*, 239.

6. Ibid., 244.

7. Ibid., 239.

8. Ibid., 244.

9. Ibid., 240.

10. Ibid.

11. Ibid., 164.

12. Ibid., 286–287.

13. Ibid., 287.

14. Ibid., 94.

15. Chhāndogya Upanishad 7.1.3, trans. W.F. Sands.

16. *Maharishi Mahesh Yogi on the Bhagavad-Gita*, 332.

17. Ibid., 319–20.

18. S.I. Nidich, "A Study of the Relationship of the Transcendental Meditation Program to Kohlberg's Stages of Moral Reasoning," *Dissertation Abstracts International* 36(7) (1976).

19. V.A. Barnes, L.B. Bauza, and F.A. Treiber, "Impact of Stress Reduction on Negative School Behavior in Adolescents," *Health and Quality of Life Outcomes*, 1(1) (2003):10.

20. A.I. Abrams and L.M. Siegel, "The Transcendental Meditation Program and Rehabilitation at Folsom State Prison: A Cross-Validation Study," *Criminal Justice and Behavior* 5(1) (1978).

21. C.N. Alexander and D.W. Orme-Johnson, "Walpole Study of the Transcendental Meditation Program in Maximum Security Prisoners II: Longitudinal Study of Development and Psychopathology," *Journal of Offender Rehabilitation* 36(1–4) (2003): 127–60.

22. A.I. Abrams and L.M. Siegel, "The Transcendental Meditation Program and Rehabilitation at Folsom State Prison: A Cross-Validation Study," *Criminal Justice and Behavior* 5(1) (1978).

23. C.N. Alexander and D.W. Orme-Johnson, "Walpole Study of the Transcendental Meditation Program in Maximum Security Prisoners II: Longitudinal Study of Development and Psychopathology," *Journal of Offender Rehabilitation* 36(1–4) (2003): 127–60.

24. G.A. Ellis and P. Corum, "Removing the Motivator: A Holistic Solution to Substance Abuse," *Alcoholism Treatment Quarterly* 11(3/4) (1994).

24. C.N. Alexander et al., "Effects of the Transcendental Meditation Program on Stress Reduction, Health, and Employee Development," *Anxiety, Stress, and Coping* 6 (1993).

26. D.L. De Armond, "Effects of the Transcendental Meditation Program on Psychological, Physiological, Behavioral and Organizational Consequences of Stress in Managers and Executives," *Dissertation Abstracts International* 57(6) (1996): 4068B.

REFERENCES

27. C.N. Alexander et al., "Effects of the Transcendental Meditation Program on Stress Reduction, Health, and Employee Development," *Anxiety, Stress, and Coping* 6 (1993).

28. D.R. Frew, "Transcendental Meditation and Productivity," *Academy of Management Journal* 17 (1974): 362–68.

29. D.H. Sheppard, F. Staggers, and L. John, "The Effects of a Stress Management Program in a High Security Government Agency," *Anxiety, Stress, and Coping* 10(4) (1997): 341–50.

30. W.C. Madsen, "Transcendental Meditation and the Flexibility of Constructions of Reality," in R.A. Chalmers, G. Clements, H. Schenkluhn, and M. Weinless, eds., *Scientific Research on Maharishi's Transcendental Meditation and TM-Sidhi Program: Collected Papers, Vol. 2* (Vlodrop, the Netherlands: Maharishi Vedic University Press, 1989), no. 152.

31. H. Shecter, "The Transcendental Meditation Program in the Classroom," *Dissertation Abstracts International* 38(7) (1978): 3372B–3373B.

32. S.V. Marcus, "The Influence of the Transcendental Meditation Program on the Marital Dyad," *Dissertation Abstracts International* 38(8) (1977): 3895–B.

33. L.C. Fergusson, A.J. Bonsheck, and G. Le Masson, "Vedic Science Based Education and Mental and Physical Health: A Preliminary Longitudinal Study in Cambodia," *Journal of Instructional Psychology*, 22 (1995): 308–19.

34. H. Shecter, "The Transcendental Meditation Program in the Classroom," *Dissertation Abstracts International* 38(7) (1978).

35. M. Turnbull and H. Norris, "Effects of Transcendental Meditation on Self-Identity Indices and Personality," *British Journal of Psychology* 73 (1982): 57–69.

36. C.N. Alexander, M. Rainforth, and P. Gelderloos, "Transcendental Meditation, Self-Actualization, and Psychological Health: A Conceptual Overview and Statistical Meta-Analysis," *Journal of Social Behavior and Personality* 6(5) (1991): 189-247.

37. C.N. Alexander et al., "Effects of the Transcendental Meditation Program on Stress Reduction, Health, and Employee Development," *Anxiety, Stress, and Coping* 6 (1993).

38. T. Haratani and T. Hemmi, "Effects of Transcendental Meditation on Mental Health of Industrial Workers," *Japanese Journal of Industrial Health* 32 (1990).

39. D.R. Frew, "Transcendental Meditation and Productivity," *Academy of Management Journal* 17 (1974): 362–68.

40. A.I. Abrams and L.M. Siegel, "The Transcendental Meditation Program and Rehabilitation at Folsom State Prison: A Cross-Validation Study," *Criminal Justice and Behavior* 5(1) (1978).

41. C.N. Alexander and D.W. Orme-Johnson, "Walpole Study of the Transcendental Meditation Program in Maximum Security Prisoners II: Longitudinal Study of Development and Psychopathology," *Journal of Offender Rehabilitation* 36(1–4) (2003): 127–60.

Chapter 11

1. Maharishi Mahesh Yogi, *Patanjali and the Eight Limbs of Yoga*, [Videotaped lecture, 18 August, 1971, Humboldt State College, Arcata, CA, USA].

2–6. Ibid.

7. Maharishi Mahesh Yogi, *Yoga and the Misinterpretations of Patanjali*, [Videotaped lecture, August, 1971, Humboldt State College, Arcata, CA, USA].

8. Ibid.

9. *Patanjali and the Eight Limbs of Yoga.*

10. *Yoga and the Misinterpretations of Patanjali.*

11. Maharishi, *Science of Being and Art of Living*, 231.

12. *Patanjali and the Eight Limbs of Yoga.*

13–34. Ibid.

REFERENCES

Chapter 12

1. *Maharishi Mahesh Yogi on the Bhagavad-Gita*, 184.
2. Ibid., 386.
3. Ibid., 185.
4. Maharishi, *Science of Being and Art of Living*, 247.
5. Ibid.
6. Ibid., 131.
7. Ibid.

Chapter 13

1. T. Nader, *Ramayan in Human Physiology* (Fairfield, IA: Maharishi University of Management Press, 2012), 6–7.
2. Maharishi Mahesh Yogi, [Audiotaped lecture, May 7, 2007, Global Financial Capital of New York, New York, NY].
3. T. Nader, *Ramayan in Human Physiology*, 8.
4. Maharishi Mahesh Yogi, *Primordial Sound and the Mechanics of Creation*, [Videotaped lecture, 21, March, 1990].
5. Maharishi Mahesh Yogi, *Vedic Knowledge for Everyone* (Holland: Maharishi Vedic University Press, 1994), 4.
6. T. Nader, *Human Physiology: Expression of Veda and the Vedic Literature* (Vlodrop, The Netherlands: Maharishi Vedic University Press, 1994), 49.
7. Maharishi Mahesh Yogi, *Celebrating Perfection in Education* (India: Age of Enlightenment Publications, 1997), 10–19.
8. T. Nader, *Human Physiology: Expression of Veda and the Vedic Literature*, 16–18.
9. T. Nader, *Ramayan in Human Physiology*, 8.
10. Ibid., 8–9.
11. T. Nader, *Human Physiology: Expression of Veda and the Vedic Literature*.

12. Ibid., 155.
13. Ibid., 173.
14. Ibid.
15. Ibid.
16. Ibid.
17. Ibid., 444.
18. Ibid., 173.

Chapter 14

1. *Maharishi Mahesh Yogi on the Bhagavad-Gita*, 427.
2. Ibid., 427–428.

Conclusion

1. *Maharishi Mahesh Yogi on the Bhagavad-Gita*, 1

Index

A

ahimsa 152
ananda 13
anxiety 34, 49, 51, 52
aparigraha 156
Arjuna 5, 17
artha 187
asana 162
Ashtanga Yoga 145
association fibers 183
asteya 153
Atma 16, 28, 29
attachment 128, 141
Ayur-Veda 40

B

behavior 74
Being 10, 12, 19, 119, 120, 177–178
Bhagavad-Gita 5
Bhakti Yoga 174
biological age 57
blood lactate 33
Brahm 92, 103
brahmacharya 155
Brahmananda Saraswati 120
brain development 50
Buddha 119

C

cardiovascular health 53
Chinese Qigong 25
chronological age 57
cigarette, alcohol, and drug abuse 76
cognition 183
collective consciousness 78, 111
concentration 24, 121, 138

contemplation 24
Cosmic Consciousness 83, 170, 131, 134
creativity 43, 44

D

Decreased medical expenses 56
desire 125, 139
dharana 166
dharma 60, 187
DHEA-S 58
dhyan 166
duality 14

E

EEG 34, 35
EEG alpha activity 34
EEG alpha power 105
EEG coherence 34, 35, 73, 105
effort in meditation 23
eight limbs of Yoga 147
eliminating desires 125
equanimity 132, 143

F

field independence 43, 44, 45
fluid intelligence 43, 46
focused attention meditations 25
fourth state of consciousness 13
freedom from possessions 129

G

galvanic skin response 33
Global Country of World Peace 182
God Consciousness 89, 171, 175
Gyan Yoga 169

H

Hatha Yoga 169

INDEX

health 48
higher states of consciousness 79

I

IQ 43
Ishwara-pranidhan 161

K

kama 187
Krishna (see Lord Krishna)
kshatriya 6

L

Lord Krishna 6, 119

M

Madhuchhandas 178
Maharishi Ayur-Veda 40
Maharishi Effect 110
Mahavakya 96
medical expenses 56
mental efficiency 43, 45
mental potential 39
mindfulness 25
moksha 187
moral decisions 72
moral maturity 72, 139

N

Nader, Dr. Tony 177
natural law 62
neural imaging 26
Nicaragua 115
niyama 156

P

Patanjali 100, 192

Patanjali Yoga Sutra 146, 183
peace 107
personal dharma 67
possessions 129
practical intelligence 43, 44
pranayama 163
pratyahara 164
prison rehabilitation 74
pure consciousness 12, 19, 21, 27, 36, 66, 101, 104, 119, 177–178
pure intelligence 12
pure wakefulness 12
Purusha 28
purusharthas 187

R

Raja Yoga 169, 176
recidivism 75
rehabilitation 74
remaining unattached 128
renunciation 134
research 25, 31, 42, 70, 138
respiratory suspension 36
Rishis 96, 181, 192

S

Sahaja Yoga 26
samadhi 13, 168
Sankhya 173
santosha 159
sanyasa 134
satchidananda 12
satya 150
Self 12, 19, 107
self-referral consciousness 12
self-remembering 135
self-sufficiency 141
Shankara 119, 135
shaucha 157
Shiva Samhita 112

stress 48, 51
structure and function 182
sutra 109
swadhyaya 160
Symonds, John Addington 2

T

tapas 159
technologies of consciousness 17
terrorism 117
three gunas 8
Tibetan Buddhism 25
TM-Sidhi program 99
Transcendental Consciousness 13, 17, 21, 32, 33, 82, 99, 156
Transcendental Meditation technique 21, 51
Turiya-chetana 13

U

Unity Consciousness 91, 93, 135, 155, 156, 157, 171, 175
Upanishads 16, 27, 96

V

Veda 3, 177
Vedic literature 180
Vedic Rishis (see Rishis)
Vedic sound 178, 179
Vedic tradition 3
violation of natural law 68

W

wakeful hypometabolic state 33
world peace 107

Y

Yama 149
Yoga 13
Yoga and health 48
Yoga, experience of 27

Yoga in human physiology 177
Yoga, path of 19, 79
Yoga, state of 13, 23, 79, 81
yogic flying 100, 103

Z

ZaZen 25
Zen and Diamond Way meditations 25

About the Author

William F. Sands is the author of *Maharishi Mahesh Yogi And His Gift To The World*. He is currently Dean of the College of Maharishi Vedic Science at Maharishi University of Management, where he is also associate professor of Sanskrit and Maharishi Vedic Science. He completed his undergraduate studies at Georgetown University, and received an MA and PhD from Maharishi University of Management. His doctoral dissertation was on the Valmiki Ramayan and Maharishi's Absolute Theory of Government, for which he received the Vyasa Award for the outstanding dissertation of his graduating class. He has worked in various capacities in Maharishi's worldwide organizations for almost forty years, including twelve years directly with Maharishi at his international headquarters in Holland.